INDEPENDENT ENOUGH

LARRY SHUSHANSKY

Copyrighted Material

Independent Enough
Copyright © 2018 by Independent Enough Press.
All Rights Reserved.

No part of this publication may be reproduced, stored in a retrieval system or transmitted, in any form or by any means—electronic, mechanical, photocopying, recording or otherwise—without prior written permission from the publisher, except for the inclusion of brief quotations in a review.

For information about this title or to order other books and/or electronic media, contact the publisher:

Independent Enough Press
35 South Angell Street
Providence, RI 02906
Independentenough.com
Independentenough@gmail.com

ISBN-13: 978-1-7322670-0-8

Printed in the United States of America
Cover and Interior design: 1106 Design, LLC
Editorial Support: Book Architecture

All conflict stems from dependency,
but not all dependency creates conflict

Contents

Acknowledgments	vii
How to Use This Book	ix
Bedtime	1
Independent Enough	5
Becoming Independent Enough	13
Step One: Taking a Step Back	19
Step Two: Practicing Self-Reflection	33
Step Three: Making a Decision	51
Step Four: Reengaging with a Relationship	77
Repeat, Repeat, Repeat	85
Workbook	91
Step One: Taking a Step Back	94
Step Two: Practicing Self-Reflection	107
Step Three: Making a Decision	112
Step Four: Reengaging with a Relationship	116
Step Five: Repeat, Repeat, Repeat	120
About the Author	123

Acknowledgments

I OWE A DEBT to many individuals, from family to friends, from clients to mentors. In the interest of space, however, I will restrict myself to extending my official thank yous to:

Jolie, my wife, for reading so many drafts of my short stories, articles, poetry, and professional writings over thirty-five years that never made it to print and for supporting my efforts in too many ways to count. You have challenged me in life and love by being my biggest critic and the biggest believer in me. I have learned so much from you about how to love and be loved.

Dr. Nezam Afdhal, MD, for giving me a life free of Hepatitis C ... a life full of energy, clarity, and well-being. A million thank yous are not enough to express my gratitude.

Christine Allen—you will never know how much you have meant to this project, and to me, no matter how often I tell you. Your contribution to the blogs I (we) write and to the development of the theory of Independent Enough has been tremendous. This project would not be where it is without you.

Stuart Horwitz. Without you, *Independent Enough* would never have made it into print. Your theory, skill, and support

Independent Enough

gave me the push and structure I needed to get this book out. For anyone wanting help with their writing, from beginning to end, I would only recommend you. Thanks for the encouragement.

My son Nathan, for spending endless hours putting together video presentations for me, because, like my sons and daughter say, "Dad, you're anything but a techno-guru!"

The nine Beta readers who took so much of their time and effort to review an initial draft of the book. I can't imagine what it was like slogging through raw material and giving honest feedback. Your attention to detail as well as suggestions on larger concepts were of immeasurable help, especially when you picked up that I had repeated the same story twice.

Linda Trum, for being such a good friend and colleague for the past thirty-six years. You've been there personally and professionally to help me maneuver through life. Your friendship has and continues to mean the world to me and my heart goes out to you.

Myron Kantor, for being the single most supportive person on the planet. Your love, understanding, and friendship have far surpassed anything expected from a first cousin. And to your wife, Elaine, whose feedback has been of immeasurable help and who never forgets to remind me that my memory of my college years is less than perfect.

Chris Ciunci and Tribalvision for being so invested, professional, and on top of all the marketing that goes into a project like this ... thank you. Also, thanks for teaching Renan his backhand!

How to Use This Book

ALLOW YOURSELF TO read this book slowly. Stop when something "hits" you. Let it sit. Carry it with you for the day or for days. Give it some earnest thought. Some meditation. Give yourself some time—a minute, a day, or a week—to mull it over, because when something jumps out at you, it's for a reason. It's something important that you need to attend to. That "shift" you get in your mind from a word, phrase, or concept is what will be helpful when you're trying to accomplish what you're working toward. Forget about finishing this book—you may not. The object is to use it as a guide to become who you need to become to have the kinds of relationships you want. Take your time. Allow those "aha" moments to sink in.

There's also a workbook at the end that coincides with each step of becoming Independent Enough. While reading the main body of the work, you can turn to the workbook section that coincides with the step you're on, as a how-to guide to practice that step. Or you can wait until you finish the main body and use the workbook afterward.

Bedtime

I GO TO SLEEP early, and my wife stays up late. In the past, I felt rejected when she didn't come to bed with me, and she felt criticized when I brought it up. For years, we argued about it. Talked about it. Withdrew from each other. Sometimes we'd go to sleep at the same time and think the problem was solved … until it bubbled up again.

One day I decided it was time to sit down and come up with a compromise. We decided that three days a week I'd stay up late and three days a week she'd come to bed early. We were geniuses!

The very first night, I went to sleep early and she stayed up late. The compromise—*on its first day*—had failed because we had both given up something we did not want to give up. More important, we were not facing the deeper issue.

Until one night it hit me, in part because I had recently been cured of Hepatitis C and was thinking more clearly than I had in years. I was aware of obsessing about my wife. ("If she loved me, she would come to sleep with me." "She's just being controlling; she knows what I want." "I've told her a million times; why doesn't she just do this simple thing?"). From this awareness I was able to "work" on *not* thinking about her at all. Calming myself down. Thinking things like, "This is not about her. I need to concentrate on myself."

Then I became self-reflective: I realized the cause of my misery was that I was acting like a little boy who couldn't go to sleep without someone next to him. I was too dependent on my wife for my well-being. I made a decision stemming from this self-reflection to rely on myself to go to sleep. I closed my eyes, rolled onto my side, and fell off into dreamland.

The next night, I went to sleep early and she stayed up late. I started to ruminate, like I always did, but this time I was able to get the "noise" out of my head and become self-reflective. I was aware of my dependency on her and, again, decided to be strong and soothe myself to sleep. I closed my eyes, rolled onto my side, and fell asleep. The next night, the same thing happened. And the night after that was the same.

But then I gained another insight: that I was first ruminating about why she wasn't coming to bed with me. So I made another decision: I was going to watch how reliant I was on my wife during the day and become more independent. I became aware that I often asked her things like where the paper towels were, or was I cooking the boiled eggs too long, or could she pick up something for me to eat during my day at the office. Based on this self-reflection, I decided to be more aware of what I was doing and stop myself from asking where things were and look for them myself. Cook without asking her directions. Shop and prepare my own food for the day.

As I moved more toward self-reliance, I ruminated less. All in all, it took about eight months of "practice"—*getting the "noise" out of my head, becoming self-reflective, making decisions* on how I wanted to change, stepping back into the relationship and practicing what I had decided—to be able to go to sleep totally without ruminating. The issue of going to bed together was solved! I was, again, a genius! I also felt generally stronger and more self-reliant in my life.

I was satisfied with myself and with my marriage. Life was good. No, life was great ... until one night, I went to sleep early and she stayed up late and I ruminated like nothing had changed. "What the ... ," I thought. After all this time and all this work, nothing had changed! Were most of my buddies right? Does nobody ever really change, no matter how much people want to believe they do?

But then I realized things *had* changed. My love for my wife was deeper. And my mini-meltdowns were just that—mini. After a short while, I again realized the issue was mine, not ours. That was a huge change. I understood that I needed to find the balance between being Independent Enough to take my thumb out of my mouth and soothe myself to sleep and stay engaged with my wife in a loving and compassionate way. I guess life is what Sigmund Freud postulated: "From error to error, one discovers the entire truth."

POSSIBLY THE LONGEST study on adult life, conducted by Harvard University, has found that people who have good relationships live longer lives, are happier, stay healthier longer, and have more stable moods. In addition, their brain functions, including memory, stay stable and sharper longer than those of people who report being lonely or in conflict-ridden relationships.

But what makes for a good relationship?

Some say mutual respect. Others say trust. Loyalty. Equanimity. Acceptance. Reliability. Communication. Finding commonalities and minimizing differences. Love. Admiration. Spending enough time together to nurture the relationship. Humor. Fun. Security. Stability. Excitement. Adventurousness. Managing conflict. Taking care of yourself. Never losing yourself. Being yourself. Finding the *right* partner, friends, and work relationships. Remaining independent and being strong.

While all these are good, the single most important variable in having good, solid relationships is *the ability to do what we need to do in order to create the kinds of relationships we want, regardless of what others might be doing*. I have found that being Independent Enough is the way we all go about doing this, even though we might not be aware of it. Independent Enough is when we take a psychological step back from our relationships, look inside ourselves to figure out what we need to develop about ourselves, and then step back into whatever relationship we're in and do what we need to do. It's not about what others are doing; it's about what we do in relation to what others do. It's a process that allows us to evolve both our relationships and ourselves. This book describes that process.

Independent Enough

THE FIRST TIME I stuck a needle in my arm, the rush was so instant and so overwhelming that I ran to the sink in my dorm room and threw up. Then I settled into a numbing stupor that obliterated the loneliness, isolation, and estrangement I felt. It was the 1960s, and at the age of nineteen I was an immature shell of a person, unable to maneuver through the many relationships in my life. I had very little insight and self-awareness. I was miserable. I was lonely.

For years afterward, I would depend on alcohol and drugs in an attempt to break away and become independent from my 1950s-era, middle-class, conservative upbringing. Luckily, I never drowned in a puddle of water, like a drunken friend of mine, or got locked up in federal prison, like another friend. I got myself clean, and, over the decades that followed, I became far better at managing my relationships and, in doing so, found the key to my well-being. Only in relationship to other people have I discovered that my successes in life come from insights I have gained about myself, psychological and behavioral changes I have made, and ultimately learning to become not brazenly independent, but simply *Independent Enough*.

Independent Enough

Over the years, I've seen thousands of couples and individuals become happier by being able to manage their relationships better at work, home, school, and everywhere else. After watching the process of how they did this, I came to an understanding about relationships that is nothing new. That's right, nothing new!

So, why write a book about something that's not new? Just as atoms exist even though we don't see them, becoming Independent Enough is a process in human growth and conflict resolution that is always there when we grow psychologically or deal with conflict effectively. We simply don't see the process we're following. We're not aware of what we're doing that "works," only that it does work.

This process and consciously living it—changes how we "do" relationships and dispels some popular myths, such as:

1. Passion and purpose are the keys to happiness.
2. Find the "right" person, job, place to live, spiritual practice, business endeavor, lifestyle, or way of thinking, and we'll be happy.
3. Learn the art of compromise, because any good relationship requires compromise.
4. Being loving creates a loving relationship.
5. We make decisions by setting goals, then deciding to do something.
6. Happiness is an end goal that is attainable by following x, y, and z steps.
7. There is a certain way to be happy in our relationships.
8. Find our guru or spiritual practice, then work it, and we'll reach nirvana.

9. Loving yourself is the key to happiness.
10. Good communication is the key to good relationships.
11. Trust and respect are the core components to all good relationships.

These myths are only shortcuts when it comes to having the kinds of relationships we want. They may "work" when we first use them, but that's about it. They don't change us or change our relationships to what we really want them to be. They give us instant gratification, but that's why our relationships feel like the movie *Groundhog Day*—we keep doing the same things and getting into the same messes we've been in for years.

We don't realize that true happiness in relationships and in life ultimately starts and ends with *us* doing the hard work to develop those characteristics about ourselves so we can meet the challenges most relationships bring ... no matter how someone else is acting. That's an amazing thing to say, but it's true. For example, if we want a caring relationship, we often look at someone else to see if they're caring for us. But if we act caring ourselves, then we will actually lead our relationships to become more caring. Or maybe we need to learn how to set better limits as a way of making our relationships more caring. Or maybe we need to develop other things about ourselves that will create caring relationships. And what happens if others don't follow our lead? Then we do what we need to do to get out of those relationships and create what we want with others.

Becoming Independent Enough is not about finding ourselves or being ourselves. It is about growing into who we need to become to deal with the challenges every relationship presents, and to overcome the difficulties and pain that sometimes come from personal growth. It is about becoming happier by engaging in relationships in a way that allows us to maintain both enough psychological distance to remain intact and to stay close enough to have meaningful interactions. It's about how to be distant and close at the same time. By treating relationships as a mirror into our souls, into our psychological makeup, and our behavior, we can get to know ourselves better—because, as Toni Collette, an Australian actress and musician, said, "The better you know yourself, the better the relationship with the rest of the world."

Most of us already have the experience of becoming Independent Enough. If we have any level of success in our marriage, with our family and friends, with money, our job, or our career, we have followed a four-step process. That process may take a minute, an hour, a day, a month, years, but, knowingly or unknowingly, we've done it. Becoming aware of this process and making a commitment to it, to ourselves, and to others allows us to create the world we want. It's about a commitment to self-growth in a way that creates success in our relationships and in our lives.

The steps in this process are:

1. *Getting any unhelpful thoughts about the situation, the other person, or ourselves out of our heads.* This means taking a psychological step back from the problems we are having in a relationship, or when we're trying to accomplish something. It means stepping away from

Independent Enough

the other person or our self-criticism. It's not about withdrawing from the relationship; it's about creating enough distance from the other person that we can clear our heads of negative thoughts—thoughts that are not helpful, that seem to go on and on, and that go nowhere fast. We need to stop obsessing about the other person in our relationship—about what he or she is doing and how he or she is "making" us feel—as well as clear out the judgmental/critical noise in our heads about them and ourselves. For example, my tendency is to be a nice guy—very giving, but not always in a genuinely giving way. At times I give too much and later resent not getting enough back. I have a lot of thoughts about other people like "They could be a lot more appreciative" and "I've done so much for them, the least they could do is help me out a little." I also have critical thoughts about myself like, "Why do I keep doing this? I shouldn't have given so much. What a schmuck!"

Once I become aware of my inner ramblings, I need to clear these negative, biting, critical, judgmental thoughts out of my head before I can be ready for the next step.

2. *Practicing self-reflection.* That is, looking at what part we're playing in the conflict and other areas of the relationship. Who are we? What are we doing? How are we feeling? What are we bringing to the table that is making us unhappy *in relation to* the other person? Are we being controlling, unreasonable, too passive, too aggressive, too

dependent? Are we withdrawing, not listening, talking too much? Are we too set in our ways? Are we being too loving? Are we not setting enough limits and boundaries? Are we having difficulty with conflict? Are we giving up too easily? In the example where I'm being too giving, once I clear my head, it's important for me to become self-reflective and see that the problem of my not getting what I think I should be getting is not a problem with other people, or that I'm a schmuck, it's a problem with my giving at every chance I get. I give indiscriminately—too much and too often—without stopping to think about how I'm going to feel if I get nothing back, other than the satisfaction of giving. Only through this kind of self-reflection can we move on to:

3. *Making a decision stemming from this new insight: That is, we need to decide what to change about ourselves; what we need to do differently in order to grow as individuals beyond where we are now.* It's time to decide to develop those characteristics we've yet to develop in ourselves to have the kinds of relationships we want. These changes we need to make are the changes we've needed to make for a long time but haven't. If we had made them, we would not be having the difficulty we're having. Making the necessary changes in ourselves includes asking and answering the question "Who do I want to be in this situation? Who do I need to become to have the kind of relationship I want?" Again, when it comes to my giving too much, I

need to grow beyond simply being a nice guy every chance I get. If I want to be less resentful in my relationships and have less conflict in them, I need to decide to become more discerning in my giving. I need to learn when to give, how much to give, and whom to give to. I need to develop different sensibilities in different situations. Only through this kind of decision can we move on to:

4. *Stepping back in the relationship at the point where we stepped out.* That is, going back into the relationship and the world and practicing what we've decided to develop about ourselves. Once we've made the decision, we have to be committed to carrying out the change, not just in our minds, but also in the world and in the relationships we live in day by day. This kind of commitment takes place only when we make the "space" in our minds to do so. Amid everything else going on in our lives, this can be difficult. But if we don't do it, we'll keep repeating the same conflict over and over again.

So, now that I have this insight about myself in regard to my giving too much and I have decided what I want to do to grow, I can practice taking a breath before I give someone something and figure out logically whether the level of giving I am doing at any point meets the situation. For example, when I want to give a waiter a 30 percent tip, I can ask myself, "Is this warranted? Is it too much? What would be an appropriate amount to give?" Then I can give the amount I have rationally decided is the right amount.

Independent Enough

5. *Repeat, repeat, repeat.* Because relationships need to move forward in order not to become stagnant and unsatisfying, and, in turn, not to make us unhappy in our lives, the process of becoming Independent Enough is never-ending. We often operate within the myth and wish that we can obtain happiness in a single moment. The reality is that we are continually developing our well-being over our lifetime. I now have to repeat the process about giving too much, because maybe I'm not as successful at it as I'd like to be. Maybe there's more to my giving than simply making the decision, and I need to go deeper into self-reflection. Maybe there are too many times when I simply forget and give without thinking and then find myself in the same giving mode as before: giving and resenting. Whatever the reason might be, I need to repeat the process of becoming Independent Enough.

By pursuing this process over time, in all relationships, big and small, we discover that we don't need to depend on someone else for our happiness. We work through old wounds, interact with the world in new ways, improve characteristics of our personalities we need to develop, and become more mature (my wife laughs at this one when it comes to me). In so doing, we create the relationships *we* want and move away from or even dissolve relationships that are incompatible with our own growth.

Becoming Independent Enough

EVEN WHEN READING this book, you are utilizing the process of becoming Independent Enough. In order to focus on reading, you have to have taken a step back from the noise of the world and started to concentrate. As you read, you are relating these ideas to your own life. That's self-reflection. Then you'll make a decision about what you want to do or not do, before trying to carry out this decision. Even if you decide not to continue reading or to do nothing after you read this book, you've already used the process of becoming Independent Enough.

The rest of this book goes into much more detail about what becoming Independent Enough is about. It reaches into the relationships we have with coworkers, immediate and extended family, friends and acquaintances, and more. I hope it will be as helpful to you as it has been for me in both the bigger and smaller situations life presents us.

For example, one day I was walking to work and the sidewalks were icy. I decided to walk in the center of the road, where it was clearer, against traffic. Soon I was jumping onto snowbanks to avoid getting hit. You can probably imagine some of the things I said about the drivers who didn't slow down or swing wide.

But then one woman made a huge half circle into the other lane to go around me.

Within the quick relationship I had with the driver of this car, I was able to get the angry thoughts about the other drivers out of my head, look at how afraid I was being, and then make a decision. I decided I was going to be calmer and stronger. When a car approached, I would stay steady and look at each driver *directly* when they were a good distance away. That way, I could get a good sense of whether they saw me and whether they would swing wide. Once I did this, each car from then on went wide *and* slowed down. *Making and carrying out* a clear decision about how *I* was going to walk seemed to give a clear message to the drivers: "I'm claiming this space for walking, because the sidewalks are too bad to walk on. You're just gonna have to go around."

That reminds me of another story that happened when I was in my fifties. My wife and I and our three children were visiting my mother, and I was using the bathroom. After a few minutes, I heard a knock at the door.

"Yes, I'll be finished in a minute," I said.

"It's your mother," came an aging voice through the door.

"Yes?" I asked.

"I just wanted to make sure you were okay. You've been in there a long time."

"Yes, I'm fine," I said, consciously keeping my initial thoughts of her being intrusive out of my head. Realizing this kind of behavior from her leaves me feeling like I'm six years old, I decided to stay calm. (This all happened in an instant, because I've had lots of practice!)

A few more minutes passed, and there was another knock at the door.

"Yes?" I asked again, repeating the same process as before.

"It's your mother," she said.

"Yep, I kind of figured that."

"I just wanted to tell you not to squeeze, because that's how you get hemorrhoids."

"Thank you," I said, this time with a broad smile on my face. "I'll be out in a minute."

"Don't rush," she advised.

"Okay," I said.

If this had happened years earlier, I would have felt smothered and angry. But over the years I had grown beyond that adolescent boy who had to fight for his independence. It didn't happen in a single therapy session or by reading a few books. It was a process of becoming Independent Enough, one that took years and continues today. I learned how to become more independent in relation to my mother, to other family members, and in my daily life.

One Last Story

Years ago, I had a hernia repaired, and after the surgery I was groggy and weak. It was a daylong procedure, and my wife had to help me get dressed in the recovery room. Then she

Independent Enough

and a nurse wheeled me out to the car and my wife drove me home.

Once we got there, she helped me up the stairs to our bedroom and tucked me neatly into bed. As she stroked my bald head, she told me she was going to take better care of me than I could ever imagine anyone taking care of their husband.

She kissed me on the top of my head and went downstairs to make me something to eat. When she came back, she had a large sterling silver tray holding the best dishes in the house and a vase with freshly cut flowers. There was also a bell on the tray. She had brought me juice, tea, and flat soda in three little Turkish teacups; a bowl of soft-boiled eggs, which I love when I'm sick; and whole wheat and rye breads, quartered, with a dab of butter on each, along with jam, jelly, and marmalade.

She reiterated, "I'm going to take care of you better than anyone has ever taken care of their husband. If you need anything, anything at all, just pick up the bell, and when I hear it ring, I'll come running. If I'm taking care of the children, I'm going to stop and see what you need. If I'm downstairs, talking long-distance with my mother, when I hear the bell, I'll hang up and be right by your side. If I'm doing laundry in the basement, I'll drop everything once I hear the bell."

She then left the room and went downstairs. I thought I had died on the operating table. It was a dream come true. I could simply lose myself and wallow in the love my wife was showing me. I could take my time—days, even weeks—to recover.

I finished what I could hold down, then picked up the bell and shook it, but no sound came out. I shook it again—no

One Last Story

sound. So I looked inside the bell and discovered she had taken out the ringer.

I was surprised, so I called for her—nothing. With not many options left, I picked up the tray and took it downstairs, washed the dishes, went back up to bed, and slept for twelve hours before going to work the next day.

If my wife had allowed me to lose myself in her love and compassion, hell, I might still be in bed today. But she didn't. She gave me what I truly needed, which was a ride home from the hospital, a hand up the stairs, and my first meal. But then I was fine. I could do what I needed to do on my own.

You can imagine the conflict that could have arisen if we'd been too dependent on each other. For example, a neighbor of mine had the same procedure, and his wife took care of him for ten days. At the end of the ten days, she stormed into their bedroom and announced, "I don't care if you die. I'm not taking care of you anymore. If you want to stay in bed and rot, then stay in bed. It's your choice. I'm done!" she yelled, before slamming the door and leaving the room.

In my situation, my wife and I stood Independent Enough from each other by not thinking about what the other person was doing, by reflecting on ourselves and what we as individuals needed to do, and by carrying out what we decided was best for us and our relationship. As a result, we avoided the conflict that our neighbors got into.

Step One: Taking a Step Back

THERE'S AN IMPORTANT idea in science and engineering called signal-to-noise ratio, which is a comparison of a signal with the level of background noise distorting the signal—a way of being aware of the influences that noise has on a signal. The goal is to be able to hear the signal as clearly as possible, as with tuning a radio so that it's all music and no static.

I became aware of this concept in 2016, when my wife and I did a recording for StoryCorps, the NPR nonprofit organization that travels around the United States, recording interviews between two people and then archiving them in the Library of Congress. They had a soundproof trailer parked next to Kennedy Plaza in Providence, Rhode Island, to keep out extraneous noises. Stepping away from the sounds of buses, cars, and people talking, I detected a noticeable difference in the room, versus the sound outside the room. It seemed as if we were entering a vacuum. The woman directing us told us that soundproofing was very important, but even then we needed to be very careful about the movements our hands made against the table or of moving our feet back and forth, because any of that background noise could affect the quality of the signal and thus of the recording.

It is very important to be aware of the background "noise" in our heads as it relates to our interaction with others. In order to have clear signals about what's going on in our relationships, we need to clear the noise that we ourselves are generating. This is the first step in becoming Independent Enough. Getting the noise out of our heads gives us enough psychological distance from the world that we can figure out what we need to be doing. It's a prerequisite for the second step: seeing ourselves clearly through self-reflection. Self-reflection gives us a better map to navigate conflict and move toward reaching our goals in life. The problem we have in becoming self-reflective is that *when we are so focused on the noise in our heads, we cannot focus on ourselves.*

The noise we're talking about here takes many forms. It comes from our thoughts about what the other person in a relationship may be doing, or from critical and judgmental thoughts about ourselves—thoughts that are angry, obsessive, ruminating, analyzing, and attacking. The noise is generated when we try to figure out what someone else is doing and the motivations behind their actions. Noise can be blaming or criticizing or trying to change someone or winning an argument or being right. The noise may be complaining in general, victimizing others or ourselves, or psychobabbling. Or it can be the noise we generate when we're late for work and we obsess about the consequences. Noise is anything that distorts our signal—that is, any thought that clouds our clarity about ourselves and the world and that gets in the way of our well-being.

Step One: Taking a Step Back

Often when we are in conflict with another person or in a tension-filled situation, or when we're simply trying to improve our relationships and it's not working out so well, we worry. We obsess about what we think is going on, what others are doing, or how much of a victim we are. In our culture, this is almost as automatic as breathing. It starts in our families, when we try to get out of trouble by blaming our brothers or sisters for something we did, or with our friends ("Dad, really, the pot's not mine; it's a friend's. And no, I can't tell you whose it is, because then you'll call their parents!"). It might continue as we strive to get out of trouble in school or make sure we're socially accepted. In all of these situations, we learn how to focus on others or be critical of ourselves.

A few examples of what focusing on others looks like are when politicians focus more on what their opponent is doing or not doing than on what they will do. Religion that blames unhappiness on wickedness or not adhering to high moral codes. Societal finger-pointing when we collectively face a problem that is difficult to impossible to solve. We create noise in our heads to defend ourselves, as a way of attacking others to save our own skin, and to keep how we see ourselves intact (I'm good, you're bad).

The problem is that when we have these kinds of thoughts, we lose ourselves. The noise in our heads overwhelms our own true signal, which we need to hear to navigate through the many relationships we have—the signal inside our heads that is quieter than noise and that allows us to move toward self-reflection; the signal that allows us to be independent and strong. The noise we create is just an indication that we have become dependent on another person or situation for our well-being and that we have lost our way.

Losing ourselves is just the opposite of being Independent Enough. When we lose ourselves, meaning when we lose the awareness of ourselves, we then lose our beliefs and values. We lose who we want to be in a given situation and give up our well-being to the noise we've created about the world. Next, we act in ways we don't want to act—and finally, we become unhappy.

When we lose ourselves and all of these consequences ensue, we are not making logical, conscious choices that are good for us and our relationships. That is why taking a step back can be such a valuable and important first step in regaining ourselves, so that we can ultimately think rationally and make decisions in our, and our relationships, best interest.

But how? How do we take that step back?

There are two components to it. The first is being *aware* of our negative thinking when it comes to other people or about ourselves. We have to know what's going on before we can change it. The second is to *clear* our heads of these thoughts.

To get a better understanding of "how" to do this, you'll find practical suggestions in the workbook section of the book, under "Step One: Taking a Step Back and Getting the Noise Out of Your Head," which you can use as a how-to guide.

Step One: Taking a Step Back

Emotion Versus Noise

It is important to make a distinction between emotion and noise. It's fine and even natural to feel frustration, pain, hurt, rejection, loss, and any number of what we might consider negative emotions. The object of becoming Independent Enough is not to be pain free; it's to make sure pain doesn't become suffering—in other words, not to let difficult emotions become noise. After all, it is not the feeling itself, but the thoughts that follow the emotion, that create the noise. The initial emotion can be a guide to what you need to do next in a situation.

My father died in June of 1989, when I was thirty-eight years old. I was playing catch with my oldest son when my wife drove up to tell me. Initially, I was numb. My father had cancer, and although his physical health had been worsening, I didn't know his death was imminent. After the funeral, I went back to my daily routine of taking care of my children, going to work, and spending time with my wife and friends. But things had changed. Sometimes when I was driving I had to pull off to the side of the road because I was crying so much. Once, I was watching a terrible movie about a boxer. In the last scene, the boxer died in a locker room after taking a beating, while his son next to him cried and screamed, "No, no! Don't go! Daddy, don't leave me!"

That night, I cried myself to sleep. I could not stop crying, and my wife became worried enough that she asked me if I wanted her to call someone. I told her I was fine, I was just going through what I needed to go through. The pain I felt after

Independent Enough

my father died was deeper than any pain I had ever felt. My relationship with him was complex. I missed and longed for his sense of humor, his devotion to our family, and his intelligence, but he also raged anytime things in the family didn't go his way and was emotionally distant and critical. So I missed not having him and I missed what I was never going to get from him—those things I had hoped for until he died.

Even though my grief was intense, I never became depressed or anxious. And it never seemed to interfere with my relationships. In some respects the grief felt refreshing, because it felt real. Honest. My emotions, for the most part, did not turn into noise. I never became afraid that I was going to go so far into my grief that I would never come back. I never was ashamed of or tried to hide my grief. Not even the time I was talking with a friend at a local diner about our fathers and I started to cry openly (he didn't have a clue about what to do). I never put a time frame on my grief or tried to limit it in any way. My intense emotion never turned into noise.

Although we don't often experience grief in this way, daily experiences create a myriad of feelings, most of which we are not even aware of. That's okay. The problem comes in when these feelings create noise in our heads. For example, when we're late for work and feeling rushed, we think, "Boy, am I in trouble. I hope I don't get fired. I'm always late; what's the matter with me?" Or when we have a bunch of calls to make and not enough time in the day to make them, we think, "I'll never get these done. If I don't call Phil today, I'll miss a great opportunity and he'll be pissed." Or when we've had an

Step One: Taking a Step Back

argument with our partner and feel angry and hopeless and we say, "I can't do this anymore. How unreasonable are they? If I had just married my first love, things would have been so different."

Noise, noise, noise—none of which is helpful. It's more important to clear our heads of the noise that difficult emotions or situations may generate, so that we can be Independent Enough to do what we have to do.

Psychological Distance

Taking a step back and getting the noise out of our head is tricky and may feel weird or lonely—especially if we're not used to it. We may feel uncomfortable and a bit guilty for "leaving" the other person, or fearful they will leave us.

There is a story of a married graduate student whose mother used to call her every Sunday at noon to talk. This broke up her day and interfered with her husband's and children's plans. By the time she finished her conversation, the day was more than half over, and that didn't leave much time for her to spend with family. The student had told her mother this and had asked her if they could talk earlier. The mother said no, because that would interfere with her going to church. After a while, the student again asked her mother if they could come up with another time, and again the mother refused. So eventually the student decided that she was simply going to have to make plans with her immediate family and not be there for her mother, and that she would call her later in the day or that night.

Independent Enough

Reasonable, right? Right. But the first time the student decided to go hiking on a Sunday with her family, when noontime came, she felt sick to her stomach and a wave of guilt washed over her. The dependency between her and her mother seemed to come more from the mother than from the student, but if we look more closely, we can see how the daughter's dependency came from *needing* her mother to be needy and worrying about her mother and their relationship. During the hike, she also thought illogically that her mother would never talk to her again.

This kind of experience happens when we're not used to being more psychologically distant from someone and are more used to being dependent to the point where it causes difficulty. This is particularly true when it comes to family members, although it occurs with friends and even acquaintances. We have a certain perception of who we are in relationships, what our roles and obligations are. When we are overly dependent on someone else for our well-being or when others become overly dependent on us, it is difficult to become Independent Enough without feeling uncomfortable, which is one of the reasons we're hesitant to get that noise out of our head.

Gaining psychological distance doesn't mean that everything will be hunky-dory or that we won't experience pain, distress, or difficult emotions. Psychological distance means that when we are faced with these feelings and experiences, they don't drag us down, rule our lives, or create a lot of additional distressed thoughts. When we become psychologically distant enough, we become more disengaged and independent, not withdrawn and

Step One: Taking a Step Back

sulky. We become more dependent on ourselves. This is how we set up the self-reflection we will talk about in the next chapter.

Sometimes just disengaging is "enough", because what we need is just that. A sense of calm may come from simply stepping back, even as we still need to reflect on this calmness to see how we got there and figure out how to repeat it. It's when we don't step back that we can't take advantage of this pause and grow into who we need to grow into to have the kinds of relationships we want.

One summer when my children were younger, they played a lot of soccer, kickball, and baseball in the backyard. Inevitably, they broke some of the basement windows. At first, I fixed one each time they broke it by taking the broken pane out, going to the hardware store, and installing the new pane. All in all, it took a good few hours. After a while I decided to do something different.

I went to my wife and said, "Instead of fixing the windows every time the kids break one, I'm just going to put up that heavy plastic we have in the basement and use duct tape to seal it around the window. When they go back to school in September, I'll fix the windows."

She agreed without hesitation. And even though we were absolutely on the same page, this was the first step in a process that wasn't going to turn out well. I mean, everything was going okay at this point—how was I supposed to know it was going to turn to shit? I couldn't, because I didn't hear the noise.

What noise? The noise that said, "Make sure you check in with your wife, Larry. Make sure it's okay with her before you do

Independent Enough

this." It's a noise that often creates conflict in a marriage, when one partner feels it is crucial to get the other's okay, approval, or permission.

Over the rest of the summer, my kids broke four windows. I put up thick plastic sheets held in place by duct tape. When September rolled around, my wife asked, "When are you going to fix the windows?"

"This weekend," I said, without thinking that September in our house was hectic: kids going back to school and my wife back to teaching, soccer sign-ups, gymnastics sign-ups, all the do-gooder ideas coming from the school that required parents' signatures, and so much more I don't even want to think about it now. And why didn't I think of all these things and realize there was no way I was going to get the windows fixed? You got it: the noise in my head.

I tend to be conflict averse. You see, in the family I grew up in, confrontation meant angry outbursts with some hitting thrown in, as well as criticisms and judgments. So when my wife asked, "When are you going to fix the windows?" I recoiled into the safest spot. The noise in my head said, "Larry, you don't want to get into that now. It's not worth it. You'll do the windows when you can, but for now it's okay just to go along and say, 'I'll do it this weekend.'" At this point, I could have said to her, "You know, I'm swamped and so are you. Let's figure out what we need to do to get those windows done." But that's not what I did.

The weekend came and went, and I didn't even *think* about fixing the windows, much less doing them. My wife asked again,

Step One: Taking a Step Back

this time in a more stern voice, "Larry, when are you going to fix the windows?"

"This weekend," I said.

"But you said you'd do them last weekend."

The noise in my head shouted, "Danger, danger, danger! She's homing in, coming after you!" So I went into my little-boy mode and whined about there being so much to do. But, I said, I would definitely get to them Saturday because I had an opening of a few hours.

The weekend came and went, and the windows still didn't get done. But by that time, my wife was swamped and forgot about the windows, like I had. Then, September turned into October and the cool fall nights made the sticky part of the duct tape come loose. Leaves collected in the window wells and blew into the basement. My wife went downstairs and saw a layer of leaves spread over the floor. Now it was getting ugly.

What had been reasonable turned into a full-fledged argument. She threatened to do the windows herself or hire someone, and I was adamantly against both the ideas. The argument turned into who was doing more, what the kids needed, money, the house, and the validity of our marriage itself. We were in a full-blown power struggle. I don't even want to tell you what the noise in my head was saying about my wife, and I'm sure the noise in her head wasn't any better. If I could have gotten that noise out of my head and taken stock of myself, I could have found some of those seven words that are hard to say in any power struggle: "You're right. I'm sorry. I love you." And then I could have struggled with her to come up with a reasonable

Independent Enough

solution for getting the windows fixed. But, once again, I missed an opportunity for my growth and for the growth of the relationship. (Once I'm in a power struggle, it's not easy for me to let it go.)

October turned into November, and the activity in our house exploded as we started getting ready for Thanksgiving and the holiday season. When December came, my wife went into the basement and saw condensation floating in the air from her breath. I would describe what happened next, but I'll spare you, and myself, the ugly details.

It's amazing to me how this whole thing started and how my wife, or I, could have changed the process in any number of ways. I could have just done the duct tape initially and then finished the work without involving her. In fact, I would probably have done the work in a more timely way if I had taken full responsibility for the project. I find that when I "own" a task and I alone figure out what I need to do, I'm more likely to do it. I could have said "no, dear" when September rolled around, instead of the usual "yes, dear". I could have been more honest about what I was going to do or not do, without worrying about the repercussions. I could have been more understanding about what she wanted. I could have hired someone. I could have done a million other things that would have made the situation better and improved my relationship and my well-being.

Every noise in my head added to a chain of events that led to more and more conflict. The amazing thing here is how a problem that could have been fixed so easily turned into something totally out of control. The initial problem gets lost and becomes

Step One: Taking a Step Back

more about the relationship between my wife and me than about getting the windows fixed. It becomes about reacting to each other's reactions, instead about the original challenge to be solved. There were emotions flying all over the place because of our dependency on each other and our lack of awareness of being hooked in with each other in a way that created the conflict. It wasn't about the windows, the leaves in the basement, the kids or the overwhelming schedule. She depended on me to get the windows fixed, like I promised; I became dependent on her when, instead of just doing what I needed to do, I involved her in something she didn't need to be involved in. We were relying on each other to make the situation better.

Most of us don't see conflict in this way. We usually just see the end result and blame either the other person or ourselves—more noise. To create a good relationship, it's important to make a commitment, not just to the other person, but to making the relationship better by getting the noise out of our heads, which is the first step to becoming Independent Enough. That is how we grow into who we need to be to have the kinds of relationships we want.

I finally fixed the windows a few days before Christmas, when we went on a ski vacation. I was afraid that the bogeyman might come into the house when we were away. The ride up north was silent. We were both angry, and the children knew better than to say too much. While away, I finally got the noise out of my head and took a lot of the responsibility for getting the kids ready for the days' skiing, cooking, lugging equipment from point A to point B, and making sure no one got hurt. I didn't do this because my wife was angry and I was sucking up. I did this because I realized, after getting the noise out of my head, that I had fallen short in my responsibility to fix the windows and that what I needed to develop for myself was a sense of engagement and follow-through without relying on my wife's approval or input. As a result, we were able to put the incident behind us and move forward.

The cool part about getting the noise out of my head and becoming more independent was that I felt better about what I was doing. I felt more confident. More connected. Stronger. It feels good to do what *I* think *I* ought to be doing. It's true that when we do what we know we need to be doing after getting all the noise out of our head, when we do what we know is truly best for a relationship, we've also done what's truly best for ourselves.

Step Two: Practicing Self-Reflection

DURING THE PROCESS of becoming Independent Enough, self-reflection comes after we take a step back and get the "noise" out of our heads. Once we've got the other person out of the equation, we're left with ourselves and we're set up for the self-reflection we need to figure out any given situation. But self-reflection is tough to describe. We can be self-reflective in a split-second, a minute, or an hour, or over days, weeks, months, even years. This is the step that comes before we make any decisions about how we want to act or change.

You can think about self-reflection as a mirror into one's psychological self—a mirror that reflects an understanding of who we are in a particular situation, what we're doing, our role or the part we're playing in a relationship, what our issues may be, and how we need to change. Issues we have carried around with us our whole lives can get in the way of our having the kinds of relationships we want and get in the way of our accomplishing what we want to achieve. Self-reflection wipes off the fogged mirror so we can see ourselves, which can then lead to decisions that make our life as a whole happier and more rewarding.

Independent Enough

Looking at ourselves, knowing ourselves by seeing our reactions, is not about analyzing why we are a certain way or figuring out how we got to be the way we are. While difficult, it's simply seeing ourselves at any given instant in time and in any given situation. This tells us more about the situation than anything else we can do and helps guide us through rough times, as well as enabling us to figure out what we need to do.

Let's take the mirror metaphor a step further. After dressing, we look in the mirror and make sure our hair is the way we want, our clothes match and are tucked in and hanging the way we like; we might turn around and look over our shoulder or use a second mirror to see our back. Then, we take a closer look: Are there nose hairs hanging out, strands of hair we forgot to comb, any toothpaste on our face? We do this *before* we make any final adjustments and go out into the world. We're not perfect, but that's not the point. The point of looking in the mirror is to stand and reflect for the moment. The mirror image tells us something about us we didn't see before.

Psychological self-reflection does the same thing. Like the mirror, self-reflection allows us to see who we are and compare that with who we want to be. For example, most of us operate based on the myth that we need to find the right person to be in love with, find the right job, or find the right friends and acquaintances. But what we actually need to do is use self-reflection so we can *become our best relationship self.* We look inward, not outward, to have friendships and love relationships that are supportive and what we'd like them to be and to make our workplace more satisfying.

Step Two: Practicing Self-Reflection

Let's say I get into a conflict with a friend of mine. We've made arrangements to go to a Patriots game because he has an extra ticket, but the day of the game he calls and says he's taking his grandson. He says it in a way that suggests it's no big deal—the way men are "supposed" to say it: *Hey, this is not a problem. We're both men here. No sweat. You understand how it is, and I understand how it is. Talk to you later.*

But I'm pissed. He doesn't give me room to be pissed at him during the conversation or to say what I might want to say—because that's not the manly thing to do. So I create noise in my head about how he's wronged me, about how he always does this kind of thing, about what a prick he is, about how I'm never going to have anything to do with him again!

But then I take a step back and get the noise out of my head so I can see myself in the situation. At first, I see myself withdrawing, acting like a victim and criticizing him by ruminating about his lack of consideration. I realize this is my standard way of reacting in these kinds of situations. I often go into this mode when I get hurt or when someone else and I have a problem. I consider where this gets me and realize I'm working against myself, because it just doesn't get me anywhere, except for feeling worse. I realize this default mode of withdrawing has never worked in my life, and I feel childish when I go into it. I want to act differently. I want to be different. I want to be more mature. Logical. Grown-up. I want my mind to be calmer—not angry and anxious. I want to keep a relationship with him, but with a little more distance between us. I want to take a half step away from him so I don't put myself in this situation again or so, if I do, I won't take such a hit. I want to be smarter about this and other relationships, not reactive, like I've been.

Too often, our knee-jerk reaction is to say, "Screw it! I'm outta here! If he's going to act like this, he's no friend of mine." But this kind of thinking misses the mark. It's not about whether the other person is being a good friend or not. It's about taking whatever behavior is offensive from the other person and assessing our reaction to that behavior. What does it do to me? How am I feeling? How am I acting? What part am I playing in not getting along with my friend? Who have I been, and what kind of friend am I? How am I acting in this?

Sound easy? Of course not. Self-reflection can be tough. Sometimes when we look in the psychological mirror, we come up blank. We cannot glean an image of ourselves. Either we're not clearing the noise out of our heads and creating large amounts of distortion so we can't see ourselves, or we're not particularly good at being self-reflective in certain situations. We've seen others and ourselves in the same way for so long, it's hard to see anything else.

So, what do we do when we can't see ourselves clearly? The following section gives us some typical psychological pictures of who we might be in any given situation. These can be used as a guide to who we are when we experience conflict in our relationships.

Step Two: Practicing Self-Reflection

Self-Reflections: Going Deeper

The self-reflections that follow are broad categories of some of the ways we respond that create obstacles to becoming happier in our relationships. Identifying how we're reacting is, in part, what self-reflection is about. But there's a caveat. Our culture sees most of what are listed below as negative, or bad, ways of being. Our tendency is either to ignore these aspects of ourselves or to be critical and judgmental about them. But each of the categories listed is neither "good" nor "bad" in and of itself. For example, while a certain level of controlling behavior can be destructive, being strong and in control of self and of a situation can also be a way of leading a relationship to a healthier place.

One of the things Thomas Moore says in his book *Care of the Soul* is that "in our society we have a tendency to squelch what our culture considers as negative and be left with only the positive aspects of ourselves. We are cutting our souls in half by trying to be too perfect and look too good. It's hard for us to see ourselves in anything other than what our culture says is positive and good. However, what this does is *create* our difficulties. One effective 'trick' in caring for the soul is to look with special attention and openness at what the individual rejects, and then to speak favorably for that rejected element."

Look at the following categories, then, not as negatives but as reactions that may be getting in the way of getting what you want. Try not to be judgmental or critical of yourself when going through the list. As you read it, take a moment to reflect. Stop and see if any of these resonate with you. The categories are not exhaustive. Rather, these traits or actions are but a few of what you'll be able to come up with when you clear the noise out of your head and self-reflect. For a more extensive breakdown of the categories into lists of characteristics we may need to grow out of, see the workbook section of the book under "Step Two: Becoming Self-Reflective."

Now, let's talk about the five broad categories of characteristics that hinder our having the kinds of relationships we want.

Critical and Unwittingly Becoming a Victim

Usually, when we're in some sort of conflict or if we want a relationship to be a certain way and it's not, we believe it's up to the other person to change what they're doing. We see ourselves as the reasonable one and become critical of the other person. Often, without realizing it, we then become a victim of their behavior. Effectively, if someone else is doing something that is making me miserable, affecting my moods, having a negative impact on me, then I am a victim of what that person is doing. Anytime my well-being is tied to yours, then I am being a victim of your behavior.

A client who was unable to pay his mortgage and had a lot of debt came to see me. He and his wife had argued for years about their spending habits, and inevitably he would either back down from his position and "give in" to his wife when they argued about spending, saving, and making money or escalate the argument and begin criticizing her for, and accusing her of, getting them

Step Two: Practicing Self-Reflection

into the position they were in. He vacillated between "I just want peace and quiet" and "I've had it up to here!"

He reported that his wife behaved similarly. After the arguments subsided, the two of them experienced periods of tension in which they'd go days without speaking. During this time, he continued the argument in his head, thinking how his life would have been different if he had married someone else, or how if his wife had just not spent so much money on things that weren't necessary, he would have been able to pay his mortgage on time and wouldn't be in so much debt. This client saw himself as a victim of a woman he was supposed to love and with whom he said he wanted a loving relationship. But there was no way to have a truly loving relationship if he was going to criticize her when, in fact, *he* hadn't been able to be assertive or strong enough to accept responsibility for his part in their financial situation.

He came into therapy wanting me to side with him and understand how unreasonable his wife was. But the only way for him to start digging out of the financial mess they were in and to have the kind of relationship with his wife he wanted was for him to make some changes. I could help him with the self-reflection he needed, but first we had to stop talking about her and start talking about *his* spending habits, the way *he* talked about money with his wife, about *his* reactions to her in the overall marriage, and how he needed to stop seeing himself as a victim.

How *we* act in any relationship goes a long way toward determining how the relationship will be. If we want a relationship with less conflict, then we need to see how we're adding to the conflict. If we want more equality, it is important to reflect on what we're doing to maintain the inequality in our relationship. If we want someone to understand us, we have to reflect on how to foster understanding in that relationship. *We* set the stage for the way we want our relationships to be. *We* can be strong, not aggressive, about how *we're* going to act. First, we have to see who *we* are in any of our relationships.

What this client learned how to do was, first, get the criticisms out of his head and, second, be strong when his wife wanted something different than what he wanted. He saw that he was personalizing what his wife had to say about money and began to learn how not to personalize the conflict in his marriage. He also understood how he was being a victim and how he became depressed or angry when his wife's point of view seemed to leave them at a stalemate. As he became stronger, he learned how to "lead" the relationship into a better place by listening more while standing by his own opinions. He began to see his wife as someone who was actually a loving person who gave him much more in the relationship than he had ever realized, which opened him up to see their financial problem not simply as her fault, but, in part, as his issue, too.

Domineering/Controlling

A friend of mine, Madison, went one summer evening to a Red Sox game with her boyfriend, Paul, and a couple of friends. While driving and trying to park close to the stadium, Paul became a bit agitated. They were late to the game as it was, and he had gotten lost for a little while. When Madison chirped

Step Two: Practicing Self-Reflection

up from the backseat that he should just park anywhere and she could walk them to Fenway Park, since she knew Boston's streets well, Paul yelled back, "Madison! Of course I'm going to park anywhere! *What the fuck?*"

It was an overreaction, of course, erupting from his agitation and stress, but it was still completely uncalled for. Madison, understandably, became upset and waited for an apology or some sort of easing of tension from him. She waited for the remainder of the evening: eight hours. But Paul did not say a single word to her the rest of the night.

Domineering/controlling behavior is probably one of the hardest things to recognize, because if you're domineering/controlling, you don't think you're being that way. You just think you're managing a situation or being helpful or logical or strong or assertive. So a lot of controlling people actually don't *want* to change. They believe they are perfectly fine and that it's someone else's fault that the relationship isn't working.

When we are acting as a domineering/controlling person, the first step is to *acknowledge* these characteristics. We go about doing this by realizing that when we're angry, when our relationship is filled with tension and we're blaming others for what is going wrong, we're probably domineering and controlling.

Acknowledging this can be tough, because to really see ourselves in this light might be embarrassing. It's difficult to admit we've set this kind of tone in our relationship. We may feel overwhelmed at the thought of changing and be unsure what else to do.

Independent Enough

Acknowledgment is equivalent to self-reflection, to sitting with ourselves during times of conflict, when we're withdrawn or really angry. Paul needed to say to Madison, "You know, I need some space. I'll be back in a few minutes. I have to clear my head," with the *intention* of doing just that—of clearing out the noise and taking the time to be with himself.

Self-reflection comes from this space. We don't personalize what's happening or analyze anything or judge ourselves or anyone else. Instead, we take a breath, calm down, and see ourselves as we are—even if we're being domineering and controlling.

Fearful

Unfortunately, fear plays a role in most relationships. In fact, it motivates a lot of our behavior. That's why it's important to understand that dependency on others creates fear. If I depend on you for my well-being, then I will become scared of losing what I'm depending on. Sometimes we may not even be truly aware of all the fears we have, because some are quiet. At other times, they *scream* at us in our heads.

Whether it's an emotional, psychological, or financial dependency, fear becomes a part of our relationships. This is true whether it's a a dependency on someone for our safety, or a dependency on our political leaders to make our lives better. It relates to our jobs, our family members, our spouses, our children, or our friends. Fear motivates us to act in ways we think will prevent the loss of whatever we're dependent on. The problem is that when we make decisions based on fear, we can't

Step Two: Practicing Self-Reflection

get enough distance to reveal a clear image of ourselves and do what we need to do. Instead, we spend our time being helpless and trying to maintain the relationship at all costs.

Fear motivates us to act too cautiously; to be reactive, rather than active; to argue, instead of being calm and reasonable; to gossip, ruminate, obsess, think irrationally, become shy and timid, avoid conflict, and not take risks. *We close ourselves off from our optimum potential for the sake of the relationship.* We become bound by a fear of not being liked, of making a mistake, of losing money, of losing our families and friends, or of even losing our life.

One night in 2008, I was walking our dog, Maia. She was riddled with cancer but loved to go out late at night and piddle and sniff. We were living in Providence, Rhode Island, at that point, and when we were about two blocks away from home, a car pulled up beside us and stopped. The passenger window rolled down, and a man looked at me in such a way that I knew I was marked—they were going to mug me. He rolled up the window and drove about a quarter of a block ahead, before turning around and stopping while facing the opposite direction—so they could get away quickly, I imagined.

I looked down at Maia and said, "Honey, you're going to have to move a little faster, or we're in trouble here." But she couldn't. She was in too much pain. We did, though, manage to cross the street and had about fifty feet between us and them. The driver and the passenger got out of their car and started walking toward me. I stopped, turned, and faced them. Then I simply looked at them, before looking down at their

Independent Enough

license plate. It wasn't even a conscious thing; I just did it. I did realize, however, that I wasn't afraid. I was unusually calm. I just knew what I needed to do. Then I looked at their faces again and down at the license plate. I did this a few times, just standing there, looking between them and their license plate. Soon, they stopped, said something to each other, and got back in the car. I turned and walked back home with Maia.

Operating out of fear clouds our minds, doesn't allow us to have insight into who we are and what we need to do, and ultimately makes our life worse. By staying calm with the two men who had me marked, I somehow had the insight that I couldn't outrun or outfight these guys. Yelling probably would have made the situation worse, because it was late at night and deserted. Operating without fear gave me these instant insights that allowed me to make decisions that kept us safe.

How was I able to stay calm? Practice. Practice reducing my day-to-day fears, no matter how small or large they might be. I do this by getting the "noise" out of my head about other people and self-reflecting on when I am fearful. Then, as you'll read later on in the book, I decide what I need to do to reduce and/or eliminate my fear. The more I do this during my daily routines, the better I am at doing it when a situation comes up, like almost being mugged. But even these steps don't ensure that if I'm in the same situation again, I won't be afraid, or that I won't be afraid in other situations.

For example, I once went hiking with a group of people in the desert in Moab, Utah. We climbed for two hours up to Sister Superior Tower over rocky, elevated, steep terrain, sliding

Step Two: Practicing Self-Reflection

landscape giving way as we climbed and solid rocks breaking free as we grabbed them to steady ourselves. I was scared. No doubt about it. And no matter what technique I used to calm my mind, I was afraid. Going down was no picnic, either.

For me, being independent is not a perfect solution for what goes on in my head in all the different circumstances I will face in my life. But if I can face adversity and the "noise" that goes off in my head with a sense of becoming stronger and more grounded, along with a clearer understanding of myself and what I need to do in relationship to conflict, life becomes a lot less fearful and I have the opportunity to create the life I want.

Helplessness

I was walking in New York City one evening with my wife, when a young, beautiful, well-coiffed couple turned the corner and started walking toward us. As they drew closer, I heard bits and pieces of their "conversation". And the only reason I could hear anything at all on this busy, noisy sidewalk was that this woman was *screaming* at this man.

"You embarrassed me thoroughly! How could you do that? They're never going to want to see us again. How can a person *behave* like that? This is unbelievable. *You* are unbelievable! I just don't understand how one person …" She went on and on and on.

Her companion responded simply, "Yes, dear. I understand. I will try harder. I promise I will."

"But you always promise, and *you keep doing the same thing over and over again!*" She was screaming at this point.

Independent Enough

He walked, speechless, with his head down and his shoulders somewhat hunched. Why? Because this young man felt helpless. All he could do was respond to her anger and try to keep it from escalating even further. He was overly apologetic, acting childlike in his demeanor and speech (as if his mommy were reprimanding him), appeared disempowered and weak, and seemed powerless to do little more than be helpless.

What this man needed to learn was how to be more assertive and how to set limits, maybe by going to therapy or taking a class or reading materials on being assertive—something that would challenge him and help build his confidence. His goal might be to be strong enough in that moment to say, "Stop screaming at me. I'll listen, but only if you're reasonable." It might be to define what kind of relationship he wants and what he needs to do to create that.

The problem was that he wasn't Independent Enough to know he needed to do these things. He was too close to the situation and too close to her (and she was too close to him). He was so busy fending off attacks and trying to simply keep the argument from exploding, he couldn't see that the "noise" in his head was keeping him from making any progress toward what he wanted.

It's easy for us to say, or think, that he needed to stand up to her. But it isn't that simple. What he first needed was the *motivation* to change his situation; then he needed to get some distance from the attacks and from what he was probably saying about himself in relation to those attacks. His meekness, his helplessness, came from his dependency, which, again, created fear.

Step Two: Practicing Self-Reflection

The motivation to change a relationship for the better is one of the keys to becoming Independent Enough. When I was in graduate school, a professor told me that clients' motivation was the number one variable that affected how readily they accomplished what they came to therapy for. We are usually motivated to move away from something or go toward something. In other words, we have to want our relationships to truly change. We have to want to be happier. We have to be motivated to do the work. Then we can move toward having the insight about how helpless we are acting so we can ultimately make some changes.

Losing Yourself

It's your first date with a woman your sister says is *perfect* for you. She rock climbs, eats vegetarian, loves Dalmatians, and binge-watches Netflix. You ... well, you tried indoor rock climbing once, couldn't get more than two feet off the ground, and vowed never to return; you love the occasional sirloin; you *tolerate* dogs; and you don't have a Netflix account or even really know what it does. But once you're on that date, the parts of you that don't match up with her morph and contort. You order a salad, instead of the steak tips; your second date is to the local climbing gym; you'd *love* to watch Spot while she's away in Greece next month.

Wait, what?

We lose ourselves in many different ways in our relationships. This is not necessarily a bad thing. A friend of mine

Independent Enough

once said he really likes to see his wife happy, so it's not a problem for him to do certain things or go certain places he wouldn't normally do or go. He doesn't carry around resentment or "noise" when he extends himself in this way. Some people might see him as giving up what he wants for his wife, or as losing himself and becoming dependent, but my friend is actually being Independent Enough. We know he's being Independent Enough because what he's doing for his wife is not causing him any personal problems or, as we therapists like to say, intrapsychic difficulties. It's not causing problems in his career. He's not angry. And it's not causing him any conflict in his relationships, either with his wife or with anyone else. He actually feels good about it.

But oftentimes doing for others and giving ourselves up does cause problems in relationships. If I do what I don't want to do because you want me to, and I get resentful or angry or expect you to pay me back in kind, or if it creates any kind of conflict between you and me, then it becomes a problem.

This morning, I woke up with absolutely nothing to do until I had an appointment at eleven o'clock. I wanted to go to the YMCA and work out, have something to eat, and finish editing this chapter. My wife woke up sick and asked me to get her a glass of orange juice with a teaspoonful of superfood and make a pitcher of hot tea. This wasn't in the plan, and when I went downstairs, the kitchen was a mess—something that drives me bonkers. Because I'm not such a well-developed human being, ready to sit on the mountaintop and be everyone's guru, I instantly became resentful and felt pressured to do what she

Step Two: Practicing Self-Reflection

wanted and what I wanted. In a nanosecond, I figured I couldn't do what I wanted to do, I was going to have to give myself up to give her what she wanted. After all, she was sick and that was the least I could do. Isn't that what marriage is about? Wouldn't she do it for me? How could I turn her down? But then there was the resentment.

"Buck up", you might be thinking, or, "Typical male". But it's not about bucking up or trying to be so pure as not to be resentful in this kind of situation. It's about trying to find a way to keep myself whole while, at the same time, doing what is reasonable to do for someone else. It's a matter of: 1) what I think is right to do, and 2) what I need to do for myself. First, by thinking and acting on what I think is right to do, I am keeping myself whole. I am doing it in part because my wife asks me to do it, but I'm also doing it because I'm staying true to my own belief that being kind is an important element in the way I want to live my life. Doing for her keeps me intact, close to my system of beliefs about how I want to live my life. Contrary to losing myself, I am actually supporting who I want to be.

Second, I take care of the resentment and remain a full self by figuring how I can also eat breakfast, have my eleven o'clock appointment, and still work on this chapter. As a matter of fact, the situation helped me because it gave me ideas of what to write.

If you're doing okay personally, at work or in your relationships, chances are, you're being Independent Enough. But if you're "changing" yourself, giving yourself up for another person, and there is conflict, then chances are you're not being Independent Enough.

Independent Enough

Sometimes we're so busy keeping up appearances and keeping others happy in order for relationships to "work" that we fail to keep or develop the strength, well-being, and independence we need. Maybe we're scared to voice our opinions, maybe we walk on eggshells, maybe we constantly take care of others at our own expense, maybe we constantly think about the other person over and over again until we imagine we simply cannot function without them.

Whether it's learning how to be more assertive, calming our minds, developing more rewarding individual lives, learning how to cook for ourselves, doing our own laundry, getting more solitude in our close relationships, learning how to carve out time out for ourselves, learning to know when and when not to be a caretaker, developing meaning and purpose outside our close relationships, or just saying, "You know, I don't really care for rock climbing, but you go ahead and I'll meet you later," we could all learn a thing or two about how to be with others without losing ourselves.

All the insights in this chapter are well and good. But insight for the sake of insight is foolish. It's psychobabble. It amounts to nothing more than what AA calls "paralysis through analysis". The only time the insights gained from self-reflection are useful is when we follow them up with the decision to change—or not to change. That's what we'll be talking about in the next chapter: Step Three of becoming Independent Enough.

Step Three: Making a Decision

THE THIRD STEP in the process of becoming Independent Enough is deciding about a particular change we want to make, or deciding not to change at all. This decision is what we come to after we've looked in the mirror and just before we fix that final strand of hair that's out of place. We're still in a state of self-reflection, because the focus is still on us. We're the ones making decisions about what to change, not relying on anyone else to do that. We're still deep in thought, with the "noise" of the world gone, or at least quieted enough, for us to decide on our next step.

The decisions we make need to be tied to the self-reflections and insights we've come up with. If I realize I'm too passive, my decision will be to work on becoming more assertive. If I understand I'm full of self-doubt, I'll work on becoming more confident. The decisions I make are not about "finding myself"; they're about becoming who I need to become in my relationships. And who I need to become is about growing into who I need to be. That's why it's so important to make these decisions *after* we look at who we are—*after* we've seen ourselves in the mirror.

Independent Enough

Making a change stemming from self-reflection is true change, versus pseudochange. Pseudochange means we play the same game as before, but with a different slant. Let's say I'm always the one who takes the initiative in my relationship with you, but I've decided I'm not going to do that anymore. I'm tired of always being the one making decisions, even though for a long time I've based my self-esteem on being the one who is strong enough in our relationship to take a leadership role. I've been dependent on you to follow my initiatives or, at least, to allow me to be the one in charge. Now, I want *you* to take the initiative. I've decided to keep quiet and wait to see what you'll do. In effect, my well-being is still being tied to your making the change I want you to make; my happiness depends on you. So, while I'm changing by not being the first to come up with ideas about what to do, I'm depending on you to make a change in order for me to feel okay about things getting done. I'm afraid to just change and allow our relationship to play out the way it's going to play out. I'm needing you to step up and do your part. This is not real change—it's gamey. The dynamic of "my well-being is tied to your well-being" is still getting played out.

The kind of decision making we're talking about in this chapter, in contrast, helps us become more independent in our relationships. It doesn't simply take the same dependency and change the way it looks. It doesn't take the same "need" for the other person and simply use a different strategy to get that "need" met. Real change is when we've truly looked into our psychological mirror and have seen what we believe we need to change to make a situation better, regardless of what

Step Three: Making a Decision

someone else might do. Real change is usually about looking at a characteristic that has gotten in the way of our happiness for a long time and growing past it, changing it so it better fits our situation in a way that's healthy for us and our relationship. It's what we now know to be true about ourselves. And we make a commitment to ourselves to change whatever that is, because *we* believe we have to. *We* believe that it's in everyone's best interest. *We* believe it's the "right" thing to do.

Real change is about personal growth, not in a selfish way, but in a way that is good for us *and* the relationships we're in. It's one of the reasons we're hesitant to make decisions: we're afraid of growing. Because growth is not simply learning new skills or developing different parts of ourselves. When we're in a relationship, growth can have major ramifications for the relationship, as we've talked about in previous chapters.

Let's say I'm full of self-doubt and needing to work on becoming more confident. If I'm in a long-term relationship, part of our dynamic will be that I am full of self-doubt and my partner knows this and we both interact in certain ways around my self-doubt. My self-doubt, and the other person's reaction to it, and my reaction to their reaction to my self-doubt, become part of an intimate dynamic we have created. Every relationship has this intimate dynamic. I act a certain way, you act in response, I act in response to your response, and on and on. This is part of the dependency we have created with others and they have created with us. I "know" what you'll do and you "know" what I'll do. We settle in. When I change, even for my good and the good of the relationship, I throw off this intimate dance. We're developing something

Independent Enough

new. When I become more confident, I will interact in different ways than others are used to.

Here's how it works:

Below is a chart. Let's call it the growth chart. The vertical line represents independence. The number 10 is pretty close to birth, when we are almost totally dependent on other people. As we get older, we ideally become more independent. And as we become more independent, we move from a 10 to a 20 to a 30 to a 40 and so on. Nobody makes it to 100, because there is no such thing as being totally independent in a relationship.

```
100
 90
 80
 70
 60
 50
 40
 30
 20
 10
```

You   Another Person

Step Three: Making a Decision

Let's say you (represented by "You" on the horizontal line) are about 25 years old and have grown into becoming a 50. You meet another person ("Another Person" on the horizontal line), who is the love of your life and who is also a 50, or close enough to being a 50. (If they aren't, you probably won't be compatible. Getting along well with someone who is a 20, or with someone who is an 80, while you're a 50 isn't going to happen. We meet and stay with people who are similar to us when it comes to the amount of independence we have gained in our lives.)

Everything is well. You marry. Then, a few years into the marriage, you decide you want a career change. You've never gone to college and have worked as a bartender for years. You make really good money and have a lot of fun, but it's getting old and now you want something "more", something different. You apply to college and get accepted. After taking one or two classes per semester, you decide to go full-time and work toward a business degree. Between working at the restaurant, going to classes, and studying, you've had to become more organized and you've stopped going out after work to party with the other people, including your wife, who work at the restaurant. You get up earlier in the morning, have much more of a routine, and have started to work out a little. You are changing, becoming who you need to become in order to make a major change in your life. You've grown from a 50 to a 60, but your spouse is still at a 50. She still goes out with friends after work. She still sleeps late. She still doesn't know what she wants to do in life.

As you grow, this causes conflict between you and your spouse. The emotional and psychological distance between

Independent Enough

your becoming a 60 and your wife staying a 50 creates the conflict, which can range from mild tension to outright arguing or simply a feeling of distance, like the marriage isn't going to last.

Why do decisions that foster growth create conflict? Because change is unnerving. It is unsettling for people not to know where they are in relationship to another person anymore. It shifts the psychological ground underneath our feet. People become worried that the relationship will change for them and/or that you might leave them. Nobody knows what will happen.

In the situation described on the previous page, a number of things can happen.

1. Your wife might create conflict as a way of trying to get you to come back to a 50. It may be unconscious and subtle, or it might be loud and obvious, but it's there. You might then decide not to continue your changes and revert to a 50 in order to go back to the way things were. You could drop out of school or allow your grades to slip. You could stop working out and start going out with your friends and wife again and sleep later in the morning. You could simply give up on your dream of getting a business degree. At this point, homeostasis would be restored. (I have often heard people say, "It's not worth the hassle. The amount of arguing it's causing isn't worth it. I'd much rather just keep things the way they were.")

2. You could decide to stay the course, conflict and all. You could keep growing and keep moving toward becoming Independent Enough. If you decided to continue to

Step Three: Making a Decision

grow, your wife could decompensate to a 45. She could party even more. Become depressed. Start flirting and think about having an affair or actually have an affair. She could increase the arguments, making it harder for you to maintain your growth.

If you do decide to keep growing, at this point, different things might happen:

3. Your wife could see the advantage of the growth you've made and decide to grow as well; you and she could become more mature and more grounded, having created a new sense of independence in your relationship. You could then meet at a 60.

4. Your wife could continue to decompensate, and the disparity between where you are and where she is could become too great, and you might split up. This is what happens when one person grows and the other stays the same or decompensates. Many separations happen because of this; we might blame arguing or money issues or the other person's irresponsibility or whatever the content of the issue might be. Although these may be valid, the underlining issue is that one person has grown and the other has not.

5. Both partners could grow, but in two different directions. You might become a business person with a masters in business administration who wants to go to Wall Street and make a fortune, while your wife might decide to give up all worldly possessions, move to India, and devote herself to the study of prayer.

Independent Enough

All these different possibilities illuminate how easily we can become afraid when we're making decisions about what changes we're going to make. At this point, you might be thinking, "How can this cause fear, because aren't we talking about being afraid *before* any decisions are made? Remember, we're still in self-reflection; we're simply deciding how we're going to change. And if that's true, then how do we know these things can take place?"

We have learned through previous experiences. We have learned by watching our mothers and fathers struggle with their relationships. We have learned from our own experiences with friends and family over the years as we have tried to make changes and have gotten the kinds of reactions the growth chart describes. For example, remember the conflict between you and your parents when you were an adolescent? Most of that arguing was, and still may be, about teenagers wanting to grow and become more independent and their family wanting them to stay under their wing. Or our parents want us to move on with our lives and we're resistant to that. And who hasn't been hurt by a middle school or high school relationship, either with a "first love" or with friends, or had problems with work or school? All of these experiences "teach" us about dependency and what growing is about, about how our growth affects other people, and about the dynamics that get set up when we try to change. By the time we're older, we know what to expect when we're going to make the decision to grow. We've learned our lessons well, even though these lessons might be unconscious and not obvious to us.

Step Three: Making a Decision

Seven Ways of Looking at Fear

Given all the different possibilities of what could happen when we make a decision to change and the fact that we've been dependent on others for our well-being, the potential ramifications of change make us afraid to truly change. The possibility of losing something we've depended on creates the fear. For example, if I'm a helper and I back away from helping you in the way that I have before, I change the dynamic between the two of us and I am afraid you'll leave. That the relationship will be over. I am also afraid of the unknown, because when I start to grow, I don't know what will happen. I don't know where my growth will lead me and what you'll do. I also don't know what I'll do. Maybe, I'll leave you. Remember, I've learned through the years that change can be unpredictable and it's this quality of change that can create fearfulness. This can happen in the context of a love relationship, a friendship, a job, or even our belief that the government will operate in a certain way to give us a better life. Even though we might not be aware of feeling afraid, it's there when we begin to grow.

Often, we are not aware of the fear we feel in making decisions. We get so caught up in the content of what's happening that we miss out on self-reflection. Why is this important? Most of us will not make the decisions we need to make to bring about the changes we desire, because we are afraid of the fallout. If we're not aware of our fear, then the fear drives our inaction, which keeps us exactly where we are: unhappy, even though we may want to change.

Independent Enough

Our fear takes many different, yet related, forms:
1. Fear of failing/making a mistake; unsure of our decision
2. Fear of losing ourselves
3. Fear of intimacy
4. Fear of losing a relationship
5. Fear of conflict/making a bigger mess of things/rocking the boat
6. Fear of not being enough
7. Fear of hurting others

Once we become aware of our fears, however, through self-reflection, then we can work on alleviating those fears. Since we create fear in our imagination—through our thoughts, through the stories we have always told ourselves—then our thoughts are what we need to deal with to alleviate the fear.

The fears listed above are the fears all of us experience in relationships—though to differing degrees in different relationships, and at different times—with loved ones, with people whom we look up to, at a job interview, with someone we want to impress or someone who has perceived power over us.

We operate out of fear anytime we:
1. Withdraw
2. Become overly solicitous or too loving
3. Become angry
4. Put off carrying out a decision we've made
5. Keep an eye out to see what someone else is doing
6. Stay dependent when we need to be more independent
7. Become obsessive about the relationship we're in

Step Three: Making a Decision

8. Try too hard to make things "right"
9. Worry about the other person
10. Put others before ourselves at our own expense
11. Become abusive
12. Act passive

The seven fears on the preceding first list are the most prominent fears we have in our relationships (not including abusive relationships). These fears often overlap. For example, the fear of making a mistake and failing can also be a part of being fearful that someone will leave us. However, for the sake of clarity and discussion, I have separated out these fears.

1. Fear of failing/making a mistake; unsure of our decision

Someone once said to me that one of the variables in being happy is learning how to suffer the consequences of who we are, because there are benefits and consequences to whatever we do. We have to learn how to reduce and/or eliminate our fears of making a mistake and failing in order to carry out the decisions we need to carry out. When asked to describe my ability to fix things, my daughter responded, "He can fix just about anything, but it'll take him three tries." The same has been true in my relationships. I have often bumbled my way through the tough times in my relationships, but the ability to keep going, keep trying, and realize that relationships are a colorful mess has sometimes been helpful. The idea behind relationships is not perfection. It's to continue to engage and develop what we need to develop about ourselves to get what we want over a period of time. Are we going to fail? Say the

Independent Enough

wrong things? Hurt someone inadvertently? Make mistakes? I hope so, because then we will know we're not operating out of fear; we're operating out of the courage it takes to make a relationship what we want it to be.

Example: You've been with your spouse since you were in high school. You virtually do not communicate. You work days and he works nights, partially because that's how things have worked out, partially because you'd rather not see him and he's settled into being estranged. You think, "It's better this way. We don't argue. There's no pressure to have sex." He doesn't know your business; you don't know his. You decide this is no way to live, but in one sense you've convinced yourself it's comfortable and safe enough, because nothing is perfect. Actually, you're probably afraid of making a change. If you try to get closer, you have memories of how it used to be and you don't want the hassle or the arguing or the pressure of having to keep him in mind when doing what you want to do. When you think about divorce, you're afraid of being alone. Of not being able to make it on your own financially. Now, you're stuck and have convinced yourself and others that you're stuck. It's understandable, because these are real concerns. But the fear you feel is not real. The difference between a concern and a fear is that when you're concerned about something, you figure out a way to take care of those concerns. You make decisions and work toward carrying them out. When you're afraid, you stay stuck. You may fantasize about what you could do, but you don't move forward. You're afraid of the consequences that your decision might bring.

Most of the time, when we stop operating out of fear and slowly move towards what we want, our situations improve.

Step Three: Making a Decision

This doesn't mean there's not difficulty in changing and maybe the change isn't exactly what we expected. But when we grow and don't limit ourselves to living in fear, we generally feel better.

2. Fear of losing ourselves

This includes two basic categories: 1) the fear of being smothered, and 2) the fear of being controlled.

Example: A husband and wife argue or bicker all the time. They argue about sex, money, who's going to take out the garbage, who does more, who cares more, who's always giving more. No matter what, they can find a reason to get into it. But why? They will tell their therapist and friends all kinds of stories about why, but the bottom line is that they feel either they will be controlled by the other person or they will lose themselves in the onslaught of the other person.

A young client of mine taught me the 80/20 rule. It's a simple concept, but difficult to carry out. In a healthy relationship, sometimes one person gets about 80 percent of what they want in a certain situation and the other person gets 20 percent. Then, when the situation changes, the person who got the 80 percent now gets 20 percent of what they want and the person who got the 20 percent gets 80 percent. Back and forth it goes. There's no need to keep track of this ratio; it just happens, like a neon light. When you turn on the switch of a neon light, it ignites the neon gas inside the bulb and the light "blinks" on and off, until all you can see is light. Truth is, the bulb is actually turning on and off at such a rapid rate, it seems like the light is always on. But it's not. It just appears that way. The same is true

Independent Enough

in relationships that have equanimity. No one keeps track. Who gets what moves back and forth.

This 80/20 rule is a good one to live by, but you can't do this if you are afraid of being smothered or controlled. The fear will not let you sit with 20 percent when it comes to your turn. You will feel like you're being controlled or manipulated. Your fear of being lost in the interchange between you and the other person who's getting their turn at 80 percent, will feel too threatening. You'll feel like you're not being heard, like you're invisible and you have to fight for the equality you think you deserve. When this happens, there can be no true equality in the relationship. You'll spend most of your time fighting to be heard or getting your way, and the relationship will become more of a struggle than anything else. On the other hand, if you get used to taking the 20 percent position too often because of a fear of conflict, there can also be no equality. You'll give in too often to avoid an argument or confrontation, and that will skew the relationship too much toward your partner getting their way too often. The best decisions for each individual and for the relationship come only when there's a back-and-forth of 80/20, 20/80, and most decisions are made from honesty and cooperation, as opposed to fear.

3. Fear of intimacy

Couples often simply withdraw from each other, not because of conflict, but because they feel as if they're too intimate, too close. It usually happens when a couple has had an especially close moment, like after making love or having a good, deep

Step Three: Making a Decision

talk or simply having a great time together. One, or both, parties might feel too close, almost like they can't psychologically breathe. Over a period of time, this can result in a dance of getting close, moving away, getting close, moving away. The same happens in most of our relationships in life. It may not feel as intense as a love relationship, but the coming-close-and-distancing pattern plays out the same way.

The amazing part of this is that, as with most of our fears, we're usually not aware of being afraid of closeness. "Not me", most of us would say. Or if we are aware of our fear, we usually blame it on our partners or other people. We say, "They're afraid of intimacy. They act just like their parents act." But what's actually true, as the growth chart indicates, is that we don't meet people who have different closeness needs.

Let's look at closeness as if we could measure the psychological distance between people in feet. If I'm a person who feels totally comfortable never getting closer than ten feet to another person, I won't be with someone who feels more at ease being five feet away. It may not look like this in most relationships, because there often seems to be a pursuer and a distancer. That is, one person appears to want to get closer than the other person. But the reality is that if I pursue you and you distance yourself, we're maintaining a certain distance between us. I may complain that you're too far away, and you may complain that I'm too needy, but we're actually working in tandem to keep the distance comfortable for both of us. Often when the pursuer stops pursuing and starts to distance, the distancer will actually start pursuing, keeping the same distance as before. Fear of intimacy is fear of intimacy, even though we may not be aware of it. But if we act in ways where we maintain a healthy distance while staying engaged, our fears are minimized and we can have closer and more meaningful relationships.

4. *Fear of losing a relationship*

This fear applies to a lot of relationships and includes a fear of being rejected or left. Psychologically speaking, all of us have experienced the loss of a relationship. We probably experienced our first loss sometime in childhood, when we expected or wanted some nurturing, loving, or caring from a close family member and didn't get it. Or we have experienced some trauma or loss of trust that left us hurting. Or we were hurt when our first love ended. Maybe we experienced the early loss of a loved one who died. Maybe we conjure up a time in our current relationship when we trusted that someone close to us would be there for us and they weren't in a way we wanted them to be. We can all probably think of some time in our past when we've gone through the loss of a relationship.

Any of these situations can create a fear of losing a current relationship. The major component for this fear, as in all our relationship fears, is the dependency we have on another person for our well-being.

Example: You're in a relationship with your boss, who never gives you credit and often criticizes your work. Additionally, he or she does not give you the kind of work that will allow you to be in a position to move up in the organization. You

Step Three: Making a Decision

feel stuck and miserable and trapped, but you're afraid to say anything because you need a job in order to eat and live. Your fear of losing your job is about your fear of dissatisfying your boss and possibly making him or her angry. It's your fear of what might happen to the relationship that leads to your fear of losing not just your relationship and your job, but many other aspects of your life (home, spouse, car, etc.). But if you stopped and cleared your mind, saw that you're more afraid then anything else and decided logically what you could do about your current situation you would be operating out of a grounded sense of self. This position gives you the greatest potential for positive change.

5. Fear of conflict/making a bigger mess of things/ rocking the boat

It is important, here, to make a distinction between confrontation and aggression. Confrontation has the potential to strengthen a relationship, being aggressive tears relationships down. Confrontation is about facing issues in a way that will be beneficial to a particular person and to a relationship. It's about being assertive, saying what's difficult to say to someone, acting in a way that sets appropriate limits and boundaries. Unlike when someone is controlling, insensitive, or thoughtless.

Many of us are afraid of confrontation. Even those who appear aggressive are often afraid of confrontation. Lots of times we won't face the issues we need to face and we say things like, "This is not a good time. I don't want to hurt anyone. She's got

Independent Enough

enough to think about without me making it worse. It's not such a big deal. I'm too sensitive." All these can be indicators that we are hesitant to confront a given situation. The word *hesitant* is interesting. So are words like *nervous, concerned, worried, anxious, uneasy, apprehensive, doubtful, uncertain,* and *uncomfortable*. While these and other feelings and thoughts may not be indicators of our being scared to confront someone, for the most part, the driving force behind them is fear. We cover up our fear using words like these to describe where we are, saying to ourselves we're not really afraid, but the fear is there, motivating our reluctance to engage in conflict, no matter how we reframe it.

Often we don't even know what we're afraid of—we're simply scared. We become so used to backing away from saying and doing what we need to say and do that it feels natural. It becomes our default. We're not aware of anything other than doing what we would normally do. That's why the awareness of our fears is important. It tells us that we need to do something different. We have a memory that, at certain times in our life, the "fear default" has been helpful, even successful. Like when you're at the company's holiday party and your boss is drunk and says something inappropriate to you, creating an awkward and uncomfortable situation for you and others, and you think, "Dammit, I can't believe he just said that!" There's a part of you that wants to stand up for yourself and say something, but because of the awkwardness, and given the circumstances, you're *concerned* it might turn into an uglier situation. You decide not to say anything and simply walk away. That *concern* may be accurate, and you do the appropriate thing. It's times like this that it's better to think

Step Three: Making a Decision

about what you need to do at a later date. However, too often we don't bring the issue up later, we simply let the thoughts of what has happened sit in our minds. We actually have a lot of these instances stored in our brain. The more we don't act, because of our fear, the more fearful we become and the less likely we are to act when it would otherwise be the appropriate time to engage in confrontation—like saying something to your boss when sober and cooler heads prevail, or going to HR or seeking advice on the best way to handle the situation from someone we trust.

6. *Fear of not being enough*

When my wife and I were raising our children, no matter what we did, there were a lot of people (family and friends) who had different ideas of what we *should* be doing. It got to the point that when I talked to my mother and father long-distance and they asked me how our kids were doing, I'd say, "Fine. They're doing really well." My sons and daughter could have had triple pneumonia, and I would have said the same thing. That's because no matter what I said or did, when it came to my children, it was never enough—never the "right" thing to do.

In addition, well-meaning friends often gave me "suggestions" about how I needed to potty train my kids or how to act to raise healthy and respectful boys, and on and on. Once, I wrote an article on "potty training" and my mother-in-law said, "Yes, that was a good article, but I guess some of us don't practice what we preach." Ouch.

Given the fact that raising children has one hell of a steep learning curve, initially, I never felt like a good enough parent.

Independent Enough

As my kids got older and moved into adolescence, I *really* felt like I was not a good enough parent. Then, when they grew up and went through the ups and downs of adulthood, I would relate a certain characteristic of mine or a particular way I had parented them to certain problems they were having. Ultimately, I was left with the idea that I was not enough.

A lot of us do this same sort of thing when our relationships aren't turning out the way we want them to. We become critical of ourselves or may become critical of others. Either way, we're operating from not feeling or thinking we're good enough. We blame either ourselves or others. Along with a history of childhood criticisms, school difficulties, trauma, job setbacks, and other relationship problems, we develop the fear of not being enough. This fear can often leave us quiet when we could be speaking up, withdrawn when we need to come closer, self-critical when we could use confidence, and can inhibit solutions when we could be moving toward growth and resolution.

By the way, as my sons and daughter grew into adulthood they each told me what good parents we had been. Which is the case for most of us when we're not feeling good enough. Even though we make mistakes, we are probably good enough to handle the challenges in our lives.

7. *Fear of hurting others*

It is impossible to be in a close relationship without hurting the other person. I'm not talking about intentionally hurting someone, but to absolutely never hurt someone you're close to is impossible. If our primary goal is not to hurt someone, then

Step Three: Making a Decision

we're operating out of this fear. This doesn't mean we can't be nice, kind, considerate, or compassionate. All of these are great qualities to strive for and to carry out. But if we stop and think about the number of interactions we have with other people, if our overriding concern is to make sure we don't hurt someone, then we probably won't be assertive or set appropriate limits or have difficult conversations we need to have.

Example: A couple came into therapy and was making good progress. She was speaking up more, and he was responding politely to her. They seemed pretty happy up to a point; then they leveled off—meaning they were not willing to address the issue of their sexuality, even though they talked about it in the session. There was no movement at home. They discussed the need to have an intimate relationship outside the bedroom but never followed up on that. Then, after months of going nowhere, the husband talked about how he had given up on the relationship. He wasn't angry or resentful; he had simply stopped trying to get close. He had accepted the fact that they were going to be like roommates. The romance, for him, was gone. He was numb. He did what he needed to do to run the household and be decent, but he had no desire to do anything else. He had accepted that the way their relationship was was the way it was going to be. His wife agreed.

They both said it was a sad session, but it was something they had both been feeling and thinking for a while. When I asked them why neither one of them had said something before, they said they didn't want to hurt the other one. Both were sad. But, during the two weeks between that session and the next, they became more engaged, talked more, and spent more time together. They had moved forward. Whether they ultimately stay together or get divorced is up in the air, but, at the very least, the husband's courage to take the risk and hurt his wife moved their relationship forward.

What to Do

Now that we've described some of the basic relationship fears, what do we do about them?

Face them.

Facing our fears is not simply about plowing through them. For example, if we are afraid of telling someone that what they are doing is unacceptable and we simply go up to them, even though we're nervous, and blurt out, "I have something to tell you: I don't like the way you're treating me," without doing the "work" first, we're not likely to get the results we want. This is not war. It's not about feeling the fear and charging forward. It's about growing beyond our fear. It's about reaching beyond where we currently are and becoming more independent so we're not so reliant on the other person to say or do the right thing so we'll feel better. It's about first being aware of the fear and asking ourselves, "How can I be less dependent on this person? What can I do to be whole, regardless of what they do?"

The fears described above are all fears deriving from dependency. The more independent we can become, the less fearful we can be and the more we'll be able to do and say what we need to do and say. If I, for example, am afraid of not being good enough when it comes to how I talk with you, and the

Step Three: Making a Decision

discussions we get into leave me feeling less than you, I don't necessarily have to work on my confidence level when it comes to talking with you. I can try to accomplish other things in my life that will challenge me and help me grow. Like cooking. If I have been reliant on you to cook for me, then I can decide to do it on my own. If I do it on my own or with the help of recipe books, food shows, and maybe even a class, this movement toward getting over my fear of cooking, of trying something I am not comfortable with and doing it independently, will help with my overall fear of not being enough. But if I take on this new project and I rely on the person with whom I am fearful of not being enough, then I haven't accomplished much at all. The idea is to become more independent. More self-reliant.

The other alternative is that I can change the way I discuss things with you. I can become more assertive, or more knowledgeable in areas we usually talk about. Maybe I decide to come up with the topics we talk about, instead of waiting for you to begin conversations. The key issue is that I move toward becoming more independent by facing my fears in a meaningful way that strengthens me and challenges me and allows me to grow beyond where I am now. As Ralph Waldo Emerson wrote, "May you always do what you're afraid to do."

A Sense of Freedom

Let's wrap all of the above into one story.

I tried to write and publish for more than thirty years. I wrote thousands of pages. Fiction, nonfiction, memoir pieces, short stories and short short stories, plays, professional articles,

Independent Enough

poetry, haikus, bukus, and hookus—you name it, I tried to write it and get published. And never once did I get anything past my desk or my computer screen.

Then I was cured of Hepatitis C and began to get serious about writing a book on relationships. I've spent years professionally and personally helping others with their relationships and working on mine. Once I was clear of the virus, I had more energy, I took fewer naps, I could think more clearly, and, as a lot of my older friends were aging into retirement with dreams of not working, traveling, and playing golf, I was catching a second wind and wanting to do more. I *felt*, for the first time in my life, that I was ready to write a book for publication. I thought the main reason I had never published anything before was that I had carried around a disabling virus for more than forty years. Now, I was ready.

I started working with a ghostwriter. I hired a PR firm. I wrote blog posts. I set up social media accounts on Facebook, Twitter, and Instagram. I wrote articles for publication on sites like the *Huffington Post*, *Everyday Power Blog* and *NAMI*. I was mentioned in dozens of articles on relationships in publications like *Redbook*, the *Boston Globe* and the *Chicago Tribune*.

After I'd been working with these other people for more than a year, the book was no further along than it had been in the past thirty years. I had spent a ton of money and had very few results. So I left the PR firm and stopped working with my writing coaches and ghostwriters. Then I ran into a man who was a published author, ghostwriter, and editor: Stuart Horwitz. His first assignment was for me to give him all the material I had written that I thought highlighted my theory on relationships.

Step Three: Making a Decision

He read it all and cut out about twenty pages, before handing the mess back to me with the instructions to cut up all the stories and theory I had and place them into "buckets." These buckets would be the equivalent of chapters. There were eight of them.

I did exactly as he said and gave them back to him. Within a short time, he e-mailed me with a time for us to meet. I didn't reply. After a long time, he wrote me another e-mail. This one basically said, "What the fuck?"

It hit me like a bat. Here was a great opportunity for me to finally get something published. I was further along in the process than I had ever been in my life, but I was dragging my feet. What was this about? First, I realized it had never been about the virus I had carried with me for years. Although the Hep C might have made things more difficult, it wasn't the cause of my inaction. I realized the true causes were my fears of failing, of making mistakes, and of not being enough. I didn't think I had what it took to really be successful. I thought I wouldn't be strong enough to get into the public eye and that I didn't have the personality to go national. I was also worried about how this would affect my marriage of more than thirty years. I was irrationally afraid that if I moved toward my goal, I might die before I reached it and would have wasted a lot of money and left my wife with less (I said it was irrational!). I was afraid because I didn't know how this was going to change my life. This was a life dream of mine—suppose I got published and it went nowhere? Then what purpose would I have? I feared facing critics of my theory, people who were smarter than I was, who would poke holes in my theory and be ultracritical.

Independent Enough

All these fears were unknown to me until I got Stuart's e-mail, took a step back, and saw what I was thinking and who I was being in relation to the dream I had. I made the decision to work on getting stronger, being more confident, knowing that I could live long enough to be published and deal with whatever might come along in my marriage. The result: I e-mailed him back and continued working on the book.

Sometimes, deciding to change can be liberating. It can fill us with hope and a sense of maturity, of being grown-up, like we are in control of our own lives. This happens because most decisions that come from real self-reflection create a sense of freedom—like our chains have been broken.

That is how we know we have encountered a real decision based on taking a step back and a period of self-reflection. Psuedodecisions, those made without self-reflection, feel the opposite: they feel hollow and reactive. Such reactive decisions will escalate conflict, create more tension, increase anxiety and depression, steep the situation further in drama, repeat old unhealthy patterns, keep relationships stagnant, bring about angry and hurtful separations, be at the core of disrespectful behavior, and solidify our dependency.

Relationships either become stronger and more functional or become such a pain in the neck that they feel like weights in our life—like trying to run a fifty-yard dash with a bus tied to our waist. It is important to make real decisions that come from true insights about ourselves before we go on to the next step of becoming Independent Enough, which is putting those decisions into action and reengaging with our relationships.

Step Four: Reengaging with a Relationship

THIS CHAPTER IS about a specific call to action. It's about stepping back into a relationship at the point where we stepped out, to practice what we've decided to develop about ourselves.

If we figure out that we withdraw when there's a problem in our relationship and we've decided we want to stay and persist through problems, the next time a conflict arises is the best time to "practice" our persistence. If we realize we come home tired and cranky and have a tendency to be critical and we've decided to be uncritical, the best time to practice being uncritical is when we come home and we're tired (we may want to prepare ourselves on the ride home). If we get depressed when our wife doesn't come to sleep with us and we've become aware of our dependence on her and want to become more independent, we can take any opportunity when we'd normally be dependent and be more independent. If we've become aware that we feel overly hurt and sensitive when we ask for something and don't get it and we've made the decision to be stronger, then the next time we're feeling rejected, we can use it as an opportunity to be rational and logical about how normal it is to be disappointed in relationships.

Reengagement is hard, because that's where we meet the world. That's where whatever we've been thinking comes into play. We may have had great insights during our period of self-reflection, we may have decided to put in place some spectacularly brilliant ideas, but once we go out into the world, what happens will test our resolve in following through on what we've pledged to do differently. What we imagined might happen usually doesn't. That is, the picture we have in our brain of how the other person is going to react is not usually the way anyone is going to react. But that's only part of the difficulty in moving from ideas into action.

Change Is Hard

THERE ARE A number of reasons why it is hard to carry out the decisions we make. First, there is how we react internally to change. When we try to carry out the changes we've decided to make in our relationships, we might feel uncomfortable, weird, or not like ourselves; we might feel like we're faking it. But becoming happier than we are now is not about being ourselves—at least the selves that we are now. Instead, growing into who we want to be is about developing characteristics that are new and likely out of our comfort zone.

A feeling of loss can accompany this evolution. We might feel like we're losing a way of being that we've engaged in for a long time. Even if a behavior is not appealing to us or working particularly well in our lives, we're used to being that way. For example, I may decide to give up depending on others to

Step Four: Reengaging with a Relationship

define for me what I think is right or wrong, and this may feel like I'm losing support from someone close to me, or I may feel like I'm losing that relationship altogether. If I have always been the "giver" and I make a decision to change that, I might feel similarly, like I am losing important pieces of some close relationships. Or if I'm dependent on smoking pot on a daily basis and that habit is interfering with my relationships, I may decide to give that up and develop different ways of getting along. But when I quit, I will definitely feel a loss.

In these kinds of situations, we're letting go of old habits and old ways of being, but we don't necessarily have to feel like we're losing parts of ourselves. Instead, we might consider that we're adding new characteristics and skills to our repertoire. Abraham Heschel, a theologian from the mid-1900s, stated that in order to be happy we need to develop different sensibilities to different situations. Another way of saying this is we need to use different ways of thinking and behaving according to whatever situation we're faced with. We may have to learn how to be more assertive with our spouse but to stay quiet and reserved when it comes to interacting with our fellow church congregants. We may decide to develop more leadership qualities when it comes to starting our own business, while in our personal life we remain an equal part of our circle of friends. If we're basically introverted and this has been a problem because we feel isolated and lonely, we'll need to develop social skills and a thicker skin while also maintaining periods of solitude. We don't necessarily have to give up who we've been our whole lives; we just may have to add to our toolbox, rather than using "all or nothing" thinking.

Independent Enough

Our second aversion to change might be that it triggers our fears, as we've mentioned before, from past experiences. This is equivalent to anticipatory anxiety or generalized anxiety, where we worry about what might happen in the future, sometimes without knowing the anxiety is coming from past experiences. We scare ourselves more than anything else scares us. Our imagination creates scenarios of what might happen: people leaving us, someone getting hurt, us hurting someone else, or just the simple fear of the unknown—the proverbial monster in the closet. We're afraid of what others might do when we change. We're afraid of what we don't know. For example, if we've tried something before and failed, future change can create huge amounts of uncertainty.

A third reason why carrying out the changes we decide to make is difficult is that we don't know what we're doing. How do we become more assertive? What are the steps we need to take to quit our job and find a better one? How do we secure a role that is right for us? What do we need to do to become Independent Enough? How can we make more money? Start a business? Meet new friends? These are the "hows" of going about change. It's one thing to decide you want to learn how to dunk a basketball; it's a whole other thing to actually do it.

There's another interesting reason why change is hard. Most of us talk about our ideas—what we're going to do and how we're going to do it. We're proud of the idea we've come up with—it's a damn good one! We get a mental boost when we decide to change, which is the positive side of growth. Whenever we move forward in life, or even when we've simply made the decision to move forward in our life, we feel pretty accomplished. And that's where the problem lies.

Step Four: Reengaging with a Relationship

Derek Sivers gave a talk at TEDGlobal 2010 in which he made the point that "telling someone your goals makes them less likely to happen". He quoted Kurt Lewin, considered the founder of social psychology, who coined the term *substitution* for this phenomenon. He also cited one of Lewin's students, Wera Mahler, who, according to Jillian Knox Finley, says that Mahler "in 1933 [confirmed] that occurrences, real or imaginary, feel real in the mind, when they are acknowledged by others. Social acknowledgment provides instant gratification." Finally, Sivers references Dr. Gollwitzer, who has written extensively about goal attainment. In 2009, Gollwitzer conducted research in which two sets of people were asked to write down a personal goal. Then he took half the group and asked them to announce it and the other half not to say anything. They were then given forty-five minutes to work on the goal, and, on average, the people who said something stopped after thirty-three minutes and said they were close to accomplishing their goal. The group who remained quiet worked, on average, the entire forty-five minutes and said they still had a long way to go to accomplish their goal. The latter group, through remaining silent, was more engaged with the challenges that stood between them and their goals and more committed to surmounting any difficulties that arose.

Talking about the changes we want to make, it seems, lessens our resolve to carry out these changes. However, that doesn't mean we should hide what we're doing and never say anything. There's a difference between talking as a way of getting positive feedback even though we haven't done anything yet and talking to get support, build a team, or get advice to help us accomplish what we want to accomplish. We'll know the difference if we stay in touch with our own experience. If we talk and walk away feeling pretty good, then we have probably lessened our resolve to follow through with change. But if we walk away from a conversation thinking more about the changes we're going to make, like we're brainstorming with ourselves or mulling over how we're going to accomplish whatever it is we've set out to do, then we've probably used talking to good advantage.

Therapists talk a lot, but, more important, we also listen and are very supportive. Often, after a session, clients *feel* better, but they come back, week after week, and don't really *get* any better. That's because Clinical Practice 101 teaches therapists how to be empathetic and supportive and how to build up someone's self-esteem. These are all very important skills. But equally important is the skill to push someone, or to push ourselves, to be Independent Enough so we can do what we need to do in life—so we can *get better*, instead of *feeling better*.

So, for all the reasons why it's going to be difficult to become Independent Enough and put our decisions into action, here are just a few things that can help:

- Build a team of people who can help you, not hinder you or simply make you feel good.
- Read books, articles, magazines, and journals in the area you're making changes.
- Search the Internet.
- Take classes.
- Find a mentor.
- Watch videos.

Step Four: Reengaging with a Relationship

- Follow a good podcast.
- Listen to talk radio.
- Follow an "expert" in the area in which you're trying to make changes.

Take any or all of the suggestions above with some skepticism. Don't simply get information and then try to carry it out. Stop and think for a while. What seems reasonable to you? How does what you get from others fit with what you want your call to action to look like? What makes sense to you? It's important to individualize whatever you get from the world. If you read something that suggests how to be a certain way that doesn't fit for you, either forget it and move on or figure out a different version of that suggestion that does work for you.

Repeat, Repeat, Repeat

MY FATHER DIDN'T give me much in the way of advice when I was growing up, but when I was thirteen years old he came into my room and set a plaque on my desk. It was a saying by Calvin Coolidge: "Nothing in this world can take the place of persistence. Talent will not. Nothing is more common than unsuccessful men with talent. Genius will not. Unrewarded genius is almost a proverb. Education will not. The world is full of educated derelicts. Persistence and determination alone are omnipotent."

That's what "repeat, repeat, repeat" is about: having the determination and persistence to repeat the process of becoming Independent Enough. It's very rare, so rare I've never seen it, that we set out to make the changes we want to make and it happens quickly and stays with us forever. Repeating the process that leads to real change is actually the hardest part of making any change. It's also the part where most of us fall short.

There are two components of this trend. One has to do with short-term and long-term learning, and the second has to do with when the picture in our heads of how our change will go in the real world is not how it goes.

Short-Term and Long-Term Learning

When we accomplish what we set out to accomplish we figure, "Well, that's it. I fixed the problem" or, "I did what I set out to do, so I'm all set". That's because there are times when carrying out our decisions seems easy. That has to do with our short-term ability to learn new skills. Some call it beginner's luck. Maybe it was simply the right time to make the change. That is, we were ready and so were the people around us. And we're pretty proud of ourselves. We pat ourselves on the back, feeling good that we have done what we set out to do and our relationship is better. We also feel pretty confident, like we really understand something we didn't understand before. We have taken what feels like a huge leap forward.

But then, when a situation comes up where we can use that change again, it seems to be gone. We flip back into our former default mode, acting like we did before we made the change. It's as if we've accomplished nothing. It can be frustrating and confusing, and this is when some of us give up.

Where did the change go?

This has to do with our short-term ability to learn new skills. It's one thing to learn a new skill; it's another to convert this change into our long-term memory. Let's look at this issue of converting short-term memory into long-term growth a little more in detail. Before the 1950s and early '60s, scientists and the field of psychology believed that our brain was fully developed and stopped developing by age six. We could learn more, but our personality and our character were who we were going to

Repeat, Repeat, Repeat

be. As time went on, the belief was that we were "fixed" in who we were going to be at around the age of puberty and into our young adult life. That as we got older we declined, or decayed, through the aging process, injury, disease, and illness. "And then," Dr. Lara Boyd, a brain researcher from the University of British Columbia, stated in a TEDx presentation, "studies began to show remarkable amounts of reorganization in the adult brain. And the research has shown us that all of our behaviors change our brain, that these changes are not limited by age; in fact, they're taking place all the time."

This is called neuroplasticity, the brain's ability to reorganize and create new neurological connections or pathways throughout our lives through intrinsic, environmental, behavioral, and neural changes. "Dendritic and synaptic connections have been demonstrated to rewire themselves via experience and, most intriguingly, through mind training," says a *Psychology Today* article by Michael J. Formica, MS, MA, EdM, titled "Neuroplasticity: The Revolution in Neuroscience and Psychology, Part I." (Another resource that delves even more deeply into this matter is "Frontiers in Psychology," an online review of neuroplasticity published July 26, 2016, titled "Neuroplasticity and Clinical Practice: Building Brain Power for Health," by Joyce Shaffer.)

Through the use of functional MRIs (fMRI), researchers have shown that we make neurological connections that reinforce our way of thinking and behaving, both negative and positive, all through our life, not just when we're younger. The neurons in our brain are connecting to other neurons in our brain and making neurological pathways. These pathways determine how and what we think and how we behave. By changing the ways we think, or by changing our behavior, we can actually create new neurons (neurogenesis). These new neurons, in turn, make new neurological connections and new neurological pathways. Through this process, we are able to actually change the physiological makeup of our brain. And that is what creates true change.

But this is not easy to do. Researchers show it takes *repetition* with *focused intention* over *a period of time* to actually have lasting results in what we decide to change. The behavior or thought also has to be *different* than what we've previously done or thought. It is also important to *believe* in the changes we're making and be *committed* to these for as long as it takes us to practice them. How long is this? Scientists say this varies person to person. We simply have to be willing to repeat, repeat, repeat ... and then keep repeating. This is the process by which short-term learning becomes long-term, lasting change.

The Picture In Our Head Is Not How It Turns Out

The second component of why repeating the changes we've made is so hard is that when we step back into our relationships and try to change, our effort may bomb, whether because there's no impact on the relationship, because the other person didn't receive the change particularly well, or because we didn't have what it took to carry out the deed. At this point, a lot of us figure, "This didn't go well. I knew nothing would make a difference. Screw it!" Our tendency is to give up and try to ignore what's going on and simply move on with our lives.

Repeat, Repeat, Repeat

The problem with this route is that if we don't take care of the "flaws" in our relationships, they fester, tend to keep coming up, and eventually lead to some sort of crisis.

Trying out a change we've decided to make is just that: trying. We're practicing, seeing what works and what doesn't. It's about carrying out the change, taking a step back and clearing our heads, and then figuring out what worked and what didn't. What we need to do next.

Regardless of what changes we make or how we decide to make them, there is always one final step in becoming Independent Enough, and that's to repeat, repeat, and repeat the process described in this book.

The process of growth, of change, is never-ending, as is the process of making relationships more of what we want them to be. Changes evolve over time, because there are certain core issues we carry with us from birth to death. They don't go away; they simply change shape. We will most likely have to repeat the process of taking a psychological step back, becoming self-reflective, making a decision, and carrying out that decision multiple times—for the rest of our lives.

Workbook

Introduction

THE FOLLOWING ARE some recommendations for how to use this workbook.

1. Make a commitment to yourself that you will take your time when going through the workbook. Impose *no* limits, deadlines, or specific goals, other than what you're doing for the day. Whatever characteristic about yourself you've decided to change, allow yourself to do that for a few days or weeks, or even a month or more. It really does take time for change to settle in.

2. Start with Step One of the workbook and go through its suggested actions one by one. Although Step One includes numerous actions related to how to clear your mind and get the "noise" out of your head, you should choose only one. Once you've found the suggestion that works best for you, practice it through the day in an unhurried way—every half hour, every hour, or a few times a day. Again, you may even decide to practice this suggestion for more than one day. Practice the suggestion for however long you need to, until you no longer

Independent Enough

derive benefits from it or until you think you've completed the work you wanted to do. Take your time. Let it sink in.

3. How do you know if a suggestion "works" for you? When you're reading and you have an "aha" moment, stop! Do not go any further. That's what you want to carry around with you through the day(s). That "shift" you get in your mind is an indicator that a certain word, phrase, or sentence speaks to you. That word, phrase, or concept is what will help you to accomplish what you're working toward.

4. If nothing speaks to you after you've gone through a whole section, stop, put down the workbook, and pick it up later or the next day. Sometimes a fresh look makes the difference. The next time you pick it up, read slowly—really slowly. If still nothing seems to be grabbing you, start over and pick any suggestion, instead of waiting for that "aha" moment. Practice it throughout the day. You'll be surprised how much something might work, even though you may not have thought it would.

5. After you've practiced a suggestion in a particular section for as long as it helps you to create the change you want, go on and try another suggestion in that same section. Continue the process described above. After you've practiced a particular step for what you consider a sufficient period of time, go to the next step and read its suggested actions. Keep going through each step until you finish the workbook.

6. This workbook is a helpful guide when you're becoming who you need to be to have the kinds of relationships you want,

Workbook

but you should not treat it as "the answer" to all of your life issues forever. Use it as long as you benefit from the suggestions. When the benefits wear away, put the book on the shelf and move on to other ideas, either from within yourself or from outside sources. When you think you might want to, pick up the workbook again. If not, let it sit until you move and throw it away or give it to someone you think might benefit from it.

Independent Enough

Step One: Taking a Step Back

This section of the workbook contains two parts: 1) suggestions that are meant to help you become *aware* of the negative thoughts you're having, and 2) exercises meant to help you *clear* those thoughts out of your mind.

First, you need to be *aware* of the "noise" in your head. This means becoming aware of the times when you're thinking about what another person is doing and/or being critical of yourself. This is hard to do at times, because we're so used to the "noise" that we're often not even aware it's "noise".

As a way of helping you become aware of what you might be thinking, the following list includes some of the common thoughts people have about others and themselves that get in the way of their well-being. After reading the list, you'll find ideas for how you can practically become more aware of these thoughts during your day—which is the first component of taking a psychological step back and clearing your mind. The list is not for the faint of heart, but if you're up for it, see how many of these thoughts, worries, and obsessions you have either said or thought:

It's not fair.

That person is being too much of this or not enough of that.

They're hard to deal with.

I'd never do what they did to me. I'm not like that.

Oh, don't worry about them. They're always critical of everybody.

Workbook

This company is so mismanaged. I could do better, and I don't even have a degree.
They have all book sense and no practical sense.
You're always late.
You never answer your phone.
You never listen to me.
You won't talk to me.
You always argue with me.
You call that cooperative?
Really?
You think you know everything.
I do everything around here.
You're lazy.
It's all your fault.
I had nothing to do with it.
You started it.
I did my part.
I did not say that.
You're prejudiced.
You're always so angry.
You're controlling.
You're abusive.
You're so critical.
You don't understand.
You're crazy.
You're just like your mother.
You're just like your father.
Your family doesn't like me.

Independent Enough

You don't discipline the kids.
You act like you don't care.
You're too tight-fisted.
You spend too much.
You don't follow through on what you say you're going to do.
You talk to me like I'm an idiot.
You're always complaining about something.
You're sick a lot.
You're always blaming me.
You think you know everything.
You don't love me.
This job is horrible.
The economy is horrible.
The doctor is never on time.
It's too hot. I hate the heat!
It's too cold. I hate winter!
They never fix the roads around here.
Crazy drivers.
Where are the police when you need them?
I can't believe the officer gave me a ticket. He doesn't have anything more important to do?
It's not my fault.
How could I possibly study for that? That test was impossible!
It wasn't me!
She's such a bitch.
He's such an asshole.
No way you're getting me to do that.
You're so unreasonable.

Workbook

No you didn't.
You never talk.
I'm tired of being the one who initiates.
I'm not sure I like your tone.
I can't stand when you do that.
Don't talk to me like I'm a child.
He gets all the good work.
If you'd stop, I'd be okay.
You're annoying.
You're being unreasonable.

Focusing on others is not the only way we distort our signal. Sometimes we blame the other person, which is projection; sometimes we blame ourselves, which is guilt. When we're critical and judgmental of ourselves, when we're full of self-doubt and dislike, when we have negative thoughts about who we are and what we're doing, all these moments are nothing more than noise in our heads. These thoughts might include:

I'm lazy.
I've never been any good at doing that.
I'm disgusting.
Nothing ever goes right for me.
I wish things were different.
I need a vacation.
I don't deserve to be happy.
Things have been too good; I'm just waiting for something to happen.
What's wrong with me that I can't find anyone?
I'm a loser.

Independent Enough

I'll never have anything better. I've tried, and I can't do it.

I suck.

I quit.

I'm fat.

I'm ugly.

I always pick the wrong line to get in.

I have a lousy sense of direction.

It's my fault.

I can't.

I shouldn't have done that.

I should have done that.

I'm a horrible parent.

I can't do much right.

I hate the way I look.

I'm not very intelligent.

I never say anything that anyone cares about.

I don't make any sense.

I don't know how to have a good relationship.

I stretch myself too thin.

I'm not creative at all.

I can't sing.

I'm shitty at math.

I have a horrible memory.

My vocabulary stinks.

I can never say what I'm thinking in a way that people understand.

I have no idea what I want to do in life.

I have no passions or interests.

I can never do anything without asking for help.
I'm a failure.
I'm not good at anything except not being good at anything.
I don't really have anything worthwhile to contribute.
Nobody ever listens to me.
I'm not like other people.
I'll never be successful.
There's no point in even trying.

1. Throughout your day, when you're feeling any kind of conflict or issue, look back at the hour or half hour that you just spent and try to recall what you were thinking (use the preceding list, if that helps). Chances are, you were thinking about another person, situation, place, or thing or being critical of yourself. Keep track of what you're thinking in a notebook, tablet, laptop, journal, phone, or whatever else you want to use. Be aware only of the number of times you've thought about another person or been critical of yourself by making a note of your thoughts. Stop trying to figure out or analyze what's happening.

Suggestion

Say, "Today, I will become aware of what I am thinking about the conflict with _____ by using a _____ to keep track of my thoughts. I will note only those thoughts I am having about the other person or critical thoughts of myself."

2. If you're not the kind of person to do that, stop every once in a while and simply think about what you're now thinking

Independent Enough

or what you've been thinking over the past hour or so. Again, focus on taking a mental note, as often as possible and without feeling pressured or hurried, when you've thought of someone else or been critical of yourself.

Suggestion

> Say, "Today, I will remember to keep a mental note when I am thinking about _____ in a negative way or when I become judgmental of myself, with the intention of clearing my mind of these thoughts."

3. Find a partner, a like-minded person—friend, therapist, family member—with whom you can check in as often as possible and who knows you are trying to become aware of the "noise" in your head. And then talk their ear off. Tell them about the situation, without hesitation, without monitoring what you're saying or inhibiting yourself in any way. Some people call it vomiting; if that's what it is, vomit away! The only purpose for the listener will be to let you know what the "noise" is. It's easier than you think. The listener has to pay attention only to any mention of the other person or to your criticisms of yourself. They can write down all the examples or interrupt you by letting you know, "You're doing it again". The purpose of the listener is not to solve anything, give you advice, or even be empathetic; it's simply to identify the "noise". For example, a married couple came to a therapy session with me, and the wife said she knew she was insecure and needed to work on her insecurity. I asked her how she was going to do this, and she said, "I need to shore myself up. Have more confidence in myself." When I asked her to go on, she said, "But if I do

Workbook

that and he doesn't do his part ... " I stopped her and let her know in so many words that this was "noise" and that it was a big enough job to shore herself up; she had no mental capacity to have him in her brain as she was trying to do this.

Suggestion

Say, "Today I will talk to _____ and ask them to be my partner, after explaining what I'm looking for them to do. I will set a date and time to meet them concerning the issue or conflict I am having with _____ _____ so they can make note of when I am talking about the other person or being critical of myself."

4. Be your own partner. Again, talk about the situation in an uninhibited way, but this time into a recording device, such as your phone. After you've finished, play back the recording with the intention of picking out every time you mentioned anything that resembles "noise". Or try journaling, which some people find very helpful. Write in your journal how many times you mention other people. Write without inhibition about a conflict or a particularly upsetting event. Don't be concerned about grammar, spelling, or any other technical issues. Just write without giving it much thought. After you're done, go back and pick out all the times you have mentioned other people or a particular person or been critical of yourself. Make the following commitment to yourself.

Suggestion

Say, "Today I will figure out what device I will use to record my story about _____. Then I will set

Independent Enough

aside a date and time to record, without reservations, the conflict I am having with this person. On the day and at the time of the recording, I will listen to, be aware, and make note *only* of the times I mention the other person or people in the situation or when I am critical of myself."

Suggestion

Say, "Today I will start a journal. I will set aside a time to write without thinking of what I'm writing or how it sounds. I will write about a conflict or issue I am having with _____. Afterward, I will read what I've written and note how many times I mentioned the other person in a critical or judgmental way or when I mentioned myself in a critical or judgmental way."

5. Wake up in the morning with a commitment to becoming aware of the "noise" in your head. Then pursue whatever creative ideas you can come up with, like creating a picture in your head of the noisy thoughts floating around in there, telling your therapist about the noisy thoughts, or doing anything else that comes to mind.

Suggestion

Say, "Today I will come up with how I will become aware of the negative thoughts I am thinking about _____. Then I will make note of these thoughts."

Now that you have some idea of how you're blaming others or yourself, it's time to move toward a third, more constructive

Workbook

option: clearing your mind so that you can make positive changes. Sometimes a simple awareness of your thoughts is enough to clear them out of your head instantly. Other times the thoughts will come back at some point or the awareness of them will not clear them out of your mind. In either case, try following the suggestions below.

1. Once you become aware of the thoughts about the other person or yourself that are creating tension or conflict, you can *clear* those thoughts. Here are some practical ideas on how to do that:

- Meditation is good ... even for a minute or two during the times you are creating noise in your head.
- Divert your mind to think about something else (Example: If you're thinking about how horrible your friend has treated you, you can try thinking about how you're going to take that class in woodworking you always wanted to take. You can also actually get involved in a task, project, magazine, movie, etc.) This idea is about thinking of something else that requires concentration.
- Divert your mind to thinking about what part/role you are playing in the conflict.
- If you've been hanging around others who feed your negative ideas, change your conversations with them. Talk about other subjects, ideas, or thoughts other than the ones that are about your negative thinking.
- Sometimes you can reframe what you're thinking. Since most reality is made up in our minds, we can change the way we think about something. This is the equivalent

Independent Enough

of substituting a positive way of looking at something instead of a negative. (Example: change "My daughter is really anxious and I don't know how to help her", to "My daughter is going through a hard time, but I know she'll be fine, because she always pulls herself up when she's having difficulty.")
- Listen to a podcast that is interesting and challenging.
- Change your thoughts into rational and logical thinking (Example: change, "I'll never get a raise, my boss hates me", to "I'm going to focus on my work, because I don't really know what my boss is thinking.")
- Be creative. Come up with your own ideas. A client once imagined a stop sign in his head and that stopped his thoughts.
- Longer term: Get into an ongoing practice like yoga, meditation, and mindfulness. Take up a new sport, set a long-term goal and start working toward it (like continuing your education or learning something new).

Nothing is perfect and clearing your mind won't be either. If you expect that you can think negatively about another person or yourself and clear you mind once without the thoughts coming back, you'll be disappointed and frustrated. This is a practice. It takes repetition over time to clear our minds.

Suggestion

Say, "I am going to get the 'noise' about _____ out of my head by using _____ (method/practice)."

Workbook

2. Divert your thinking to something else. That is, make a conscious effort to think about something else. Sing a song in your head, read, recite poetry, or do something else you've been planning on doing.

Suggestion

Say, "I will think about or do _____, instead of thinking negative thoughts about _____ _____."

3. Get occupied. Focus on something that you can lose yourself in: a project, a movie, a book, plans for something fun, or whatever else you can come up with.

Suggestion

Say, "Today, I will make a commitment to doing _____ to divert my negative thinking."

4. Make a commitment to yourself that you will try to reduce and/or eliminate the "noise" by continuing to work on being aware of that "noise." Practice reducing and getting it out of your head every half hour to every hour.

Suggestion

Say, "I will commit to staying aware of and eliminating negative thoughts about _____."

5. Sometimes, becoming aware of the "noise" with the intention of eliminating it is all you need to do. At times, the awareness is enough to clear your head.

Independent Enough

Suggestion

Say, "I will make every effort to prioritize staying aware of my negative thoughts about _____."

6. Turn your attention to yourself in a positive way by becoming self-reflective.

Suggestion

Say, "Today I will do whatever I need to do to look at my part of the issue/conflict with _____."

Once you've cleared your thoughts about a particular situation, make a commitment to do this whenever something upsets you or creates conflict. It's the first step toward having the relationships you want. Try not to skip it or think it's frivolous. Your mind can basically focus on only one thing at a time, and if you're conjuring up "crap" in your head about another person or about yourself, you won't have the attention it's going to take to make the changes you'll need to make.

Workbook

Step Two: Practicing Self-Reflection

Self-reflection is about being aware of your part in any conflict, tension, or difficulty you're having in your relationships. It's also the part you're playing when you're not getting what you want. Self-reflection is about seeing how you're being in your relationships. How you're acting. What kind of dysfunctional role you're playing. This kind of reflection gives you some idea of the decisions you'll need to make in order to change so that you can get what you want in your relationships. That is, your decision to change will be tied to your self-reflection.

Below is a list of characteristics and actions you may be exhibiting that affect your relationships negatively. The list is long. Some may apply to you; others may not. Some may not apply now but might at a future date. You can also keep this list as a reference to use at a later date when your relationships are struggling.

Critical
Hating self or other
Self-doubt
Gossiping
Name calling
Condescending
Judgmental
Dismissive
Unforgiving
Discriminating
Resentful

Nonaccepting
Blaming

Domineering/Controlling
Managing
Talking too much
Self-centered
Anger
Jealousy
Instigator of trouble
Manipulating
Argumentative
Withdrawn/withholding
Too logical
Overly spiritual
Demanding
Relentless
Rigid/cold/removed

Fearful
Worrying
Obsessing/ruminating
Irrational thinking
Timidity
Risk averse
Driven by risk of loss
Avoiding conflict

Helpless
Victim mentality

Workbook

Dependency on others
Disempowered/weak
Out of control
Martyrdom
Childlike
Hopeless
Overly apologetic
Feeling depressed

Losing Self
Naive
Overwhelmed/confused
Overly emotional
Needy
Caretaking
Lacking self-care
Insecure
Overly sensitive
Too passive
Too loving
Too giving
Getting hurt and becoming angry and/or withdrawn
Losing your voice
Becoming domesticated

The following are some suggestions for how to use the list:

1. Go down the list slowly, trying to be objective. Think about the situation you're currently in. No need to go back into the

Independent Enough

"noise"—just be *motivated* to find out what part you're playing in the problem.

2. Make a mark or write down each one that applies to you. Then go back to the items and think about them for a minute. Try to come up with ways in which the characteristics fit with what you're doing in the current situation. Be as specific as possible. For example, if you're being too loving, exactly in what ways are you being too loving? Are you always the one who initiates conversation, pursues time off together, or gives thoughtful gifts while the other person is pretty lazy about these things? At work, if you're fearful of losing your job, specifically when does this come up? When your boss calls you into the office? When you're given a deadline on a project and you're having trouble making it? When you leave for the day and your desk is piled high with what still needs to be done?

3. Be creative, and use the list in any way that is helpful and suits your learning style.

Let's say you want someone to acknowledge that you're doing a good job, but they're not going to do that. Go down the list to see the truth about yourself in this situation. Let's say you stop on *self-doubt* and realize you are doubtful about what you're doing and are depending on the other person to make you feel better. This will be your self-reflection. You don't need to analyze why you're doing it or where the self-doubt comes from. Finding out that you are doubtful about your abilities is enough for now. We'll cover what you can do about it in the next section of the workbook, "Decision

Making". For now, stick with finding out your part in your unhappiness.

Suggestion

Say, "Today, I will think about the situation with _____ _____ that is causing me conflict and take as much time as necessary to go down the list to see what characteristic or action applies to me in the conflict."

In Plato's *The Apology*, Plato quotes a part of Socrates's speech at his trial: "The unexamined life is not worth living." I wonder if Socrates understood that while self-reflection is an important element when we're trying to maneuver our way through the many relationships we have, it is also only a prelude to making a decision. While self-reflection for the sake of self-reflection may be interesting, it does not serve a purpose unless it leads to decisions to change.

Independent Enough

Step Three: Making a Decision

The decision you need to make will be tied to the self-reflection you have gained. For example, if you're overwhelmed with a situation, you may decide to learn how to relax, stay calm, and take things one at a time. If you're too sensitive, you may need to develop a thicker skin. If you're too dependent on someone, you may decide to become more independent. If you've gleaned from your self-reflection that you're being too logical in a certain relationship, you may decide to become more spontaneous.

Suggestion

Say, "I understand that I'm being_____ _____, which is getting in the way of having the kind of relationship I want with _____. Today I will decide to become _____ during those times when this is causing conflict or not allowing me to reach my goals."

Suggestion

Say, "Today I will decide to change _____ about myself."

1. Sometimes you simply don't know how to make the changes you've decided to make. I mean, practically, how does someone become more independent? How does someone get more psychological distance? You may need to do a little digging by using outside resources: take a class; google ideas; read articles, magazines, and books; talk to other people; or use your own

creative ideas for how to go about "learning" how to make those changes you've decided to make.

Suggestion

Say, "Today I will figure out what resources I will use to carry out the decision to _____."

Suggestion

Say, "Today I will figure out *how* to make the changes I need to make."

Suggestion

Say, "Today I will do _____ as a way of figuring out how to make the changes I want to make in myself to have the kind of relationship I want with _____."

2. The change you decide to make will need to be real change. *You will have to deeply believe* that what you're going to do is in your best interest and the best interest of the relationship. It may raise some fear and take some time, but your commitment and your perseverance to what you think is right are of utmost importance. You may become less victimized and more of a leader in what you want in a relationship, and this might cause some "threat" to a relationship, but it will be important to continue becoming the leader that you know the relationship needs.

Suggestion

Say, "I will commit to the decision I am making. I will believe wholeheartedly that working on becoming _____ is right for me and right for the relationship I am in."

Independent Enough

Suggestion

Say, "I will make this decision even if _____ may not agree or like it."

Suggestion

Say, "I will make this decision even though it might initially create some feelings I don't like in myself, such as loneliness or some fear of the relationship ending. But I will follow through. I am determined to make this decision."

Suggestion

Say, "I will get all the possibilities about what might happen in the situation with _____ out of my head when making this decision. I will remove all the fear—of making a mistake, of failing, of being unsure, of possibly losing the relationship, of the conflict it might cause, of feeling inadequate, and of _____.
Today I will replace fear with confidence. I am determined to make this decision."

Suggestion

Say, "Today I will live fear-free when making the decision to change _____."

Suggestion

Say, "If I have not been successful in reducing my fear so I can make my decision, today I will find the help I need to do so. I will find a resource outside myself for help in dealing effectively with my fear. That resource will be _____ _____."

Suggestion

Say, "I am larger than any fear I have. I am more than what my fears have made me believe I am. My decision to change is mine. I will own it and believe in it. My fear is no longer a part of this decision."

If you can't decide what to do, simply figure out what you need to do in the problematic situation to become more independent. For example, a friend of mine was caught up in a power struggle at work with his supervisor, and he decided simply to stop asking him about what he needed to do or what the supervisor wanted him to do on jobs he was given. Instead, he started using his own judgment and did more work on his own; whereas before he had often asked for help or permission to accomplish and finish tasks. He never figured out what part he was playing; he just "knew" he needed to be more independent. As a result, he was more satisfied and happier at work and the relationship with his supervisor was a lot less conflicted.

Step Four: Reengaging with a Relationship

You now need to commit to the change you've decided to make. You can be determined and know that the changes you are going to make are the best actions to take, given the situation. This kind of commitment is very important. The first step in carrying out the action is to believe in that action—that is, you know you are doing the right thing, and if the other person's reaction makes you want to reevaluate what you are doing, then you will. But for right now, you will commit to this action, no matter what reservations you have or how long it takes to carry out.

Suggestion

Say, "I will commit fully to the changes I am making. I know that at this moment they are the correct changes to make for my relationship and for myself. I deeply believe this to be true."

Suggestion

Say, "I am convinced that doing _____ is the right thing to do."

Suggestion

Say, "Today I will practice _____."

Suggestion

Say, "No matter what I am feeling or any reservations I may have, I will practice _____ today."

1. Sometimes you will feel like you don't have the strength or belief to carry out your decisions. You need to work up to it.

Workbook

You need to develop a stronger self in order to carry out what you've decided to do. You may need to learn how to feel afraid and still carry out your decisions. You may need to break your "larger" decision into a series of "smaller" actions in order to eventually accomplish what you need to do.

> *Suggestion*
>
> Say, "If I am hesitant to carry out my decision today, I will begin doing _____ as a way of working up to carrying out my decision."

2. As you try to carry out your changes, you need to stay aware of what's happening and how others are reacting and responding to your actions. You'll need to be aware because that will tell you what you need to do next: make more changes or keep practicing the changes you are currently making. When you change characteristics about yourself and start relating differently to people, you change the dynamics between you and them. For example, if you've always been a caretaker and you decide to let someone you've taken care of take care of himself or herself, that person will definitely have a reaction.

> *Suggestion*
>
> Say, "Whatever other people's reactions may be, I will be aware of them. I will make note of them, in whatever way I best make notes, and either make sure I continue with the changes I've decided to make or alter these changes to fit the situation."

Independent Enough

Suggestion
Say, "Even though I may have difficulty carrying out the decisions I've made, I will continue to develop _____ _____ about myself so that I can have the kinds of relationships I want."

Suggestion
Say, "Even though I may feel uncomfortable, I will still follow through on my decision to do _____ _____."

3. Sometimes you may be afraid to carry out your decisions and need support. This might be someone who will pat you on the back or someone who can be firmer and push you, a group of people who will give you support, a therapist, or any number of other possible resources like literature, YouTube videos, and so on. If you're hesitant about carrying out a decision, think about the kind of support you need.

Suggestion
Say, "Even though it might be hard to carry out the changes I have decided to make, today I will get support from _____ to carry them out."

Suggestion
Say, "Today I can muster up enough courage on my own to deal with the difficulties of _____ in order to carry out the decision to _____."

We all have what it takes to make the changes we need to make. Sometimes we don't believe we can. If this is the case, we

Workbook

need to take our time and figure out, step by step, just how we're going to do that. A client of mine once said he'd been ruminating for forty years and didn't think he could change. Over time, with much practice and, more important, with the belief that he *could* change, he began managing his anxiety in relation to other people so that he could go out socially and advance in his career. If we have the belief, the intentional focus, and the repetitive practice of carrying out the changes we need to make over time, we have the potential to develop into who we have decided to become.

Independent Enough

Step Five: Repeat, Repeat, Repeat

It's time to make a commitment to do the same process over and over again. You do this unknowingly anyway. As I mentioned earlier in the book, when your relationships work the way you want them to, you are usually following the process of becoming Independent Enough—you just don't know it. The commitment you are making now is to knowingly, consciously follow, in the many different relationships in your life and on an ongoing basis, the process this book describes.

Suggestion
Say, "I will keep repeating the process of taking a step back and getting the unhelpful thoughts out of my head, then self-reflecting, making a decision, and carrying out that decision."

Suggestion
Say, "No matter what happens, I will stay committed to continually change and develop those characteristics about myself I need to develop in order to have the kinds of relationships I want."

Suggestion
Say, "I am willing to practice the same change today as I did yesterday, in order to better myself and my relationships."

Suggestion
Say, "I may decide today to change what I need to work on, and I will follow the same process as before."

Suggestion
Say, "Even though I may feel discouraged or not know where

Workbook

to turn next, I will continue to commit myself to figuring out whatever changes I need to make to make my relationships what I want them to be by reaching out to other sources for knowledge, support, and ideas."

1. Sometimes, learning how to repeat a process can be helped along by repeating a practice. That includes exercising regularly, meditating regularly, eating and sleeping on a regular schedule, stretching, reading, walking, and doing other forms of self-care consistently.

Suggestion
Say, "Over the course of the next week or so, I will begin a regular practice of _____."

Suggestion
Say, "After a week of doing the same action, I will make a commitment to doing this action, day by day, for another week. If I have not been as consistent as I first thought I wanted to be, that is *not* a problem. I will still continue to practice regularly, no matter how inconsistent I think I am being. There has been value in what I am doing, even though I may not be aware of it.

About the Author

WITH MORE THAN thirty-five years of experience starting at a Rape Crisis Center as an undergraduate student, and finishing his graduate studies in 1980, Larry has worked for profit and nonprofit organizations before starting a private practice in 1988. Early on in his career he was involved in postgraduate studies at The Cambridge Family Institute and devoted the first eight years of his career directing a residential facility for adolescents, working in emergency services, in hospital settings, family service agencies, the court system and mental health centers. Additionally, Larry has presented workshops to staff and various organizations and educational institutions and given community talks to the wider community. He has also written numerous articles, blogs and been cited in in-print and online publications. For the next twenty-five years Larry devoted his time to a private practice where he has helped hundreds of individuals and couples in relationships. Now, after raising three children and being married for thirty-four years and being inspired by the ethereal reward that comes from helping people, he wants to bring his concepts out from behind closed doors and introduce them to a wider audience.

Made in the USA
Columbia, SC
27 June 2018